MADNESS

IN THE TRENCHES OF AMERICA'S TROUBLED
DEPARTMENT OF VETERANS AFFAIRS

ANDREA PLATE

Marshall Cavendish
Editions

Reprinted 2019

Published in 2019 by Marshall Cavendish Editions
An imprint of Marshall Cavendish International

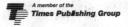
A member of the
Times Publishing Group

Other Marshall Cavendish Offices:
Marshall Cavendish Corporation, 99 White Plains Road, Tarrytown NY 10591-9001, USA • Marshall Cavendish International (Thailand) Co Ltd, 253 Asoke, 12th Flr, Sukhumvit 21 Road, Klongtoey Nua, Wattana, Bangkok 10110, Thailand • Marshall Cavendish (Malaysia) Sdn Bhd, Times Subang, Lot 46, Subang Hi-Tech Industrial Park, Batu Tiga, 40000 Shah Alam, Selangor Darul Ehsan, Malaysia.

Marshall Cavendish is a registered trademark of Times Publishing Limited

This book is published in association with Asia Media Press, a subsidiary of Asia Media International (asiamedia.lmu.edu) in Los Angeles.

National Library Board, Singapore Cataloguing-in-Publication Data

Name(s): Darvi, Andrea.
Title: Madness : in the trenches of America's troubled Department of Veterans Affairs / Andrea Plate.
Description: Singapore : Marshall Cavendish Editions, 2019.
Identifier(s): OCN 1098018379 | ISBN 978-981-48-4186-3 (paperback)
Subject(s): LCSH: Veterans--Mental health--United States. | Veterans--Mental health services--United States. | Veteran reintegration United States. | United States. Department of Veterans Affairs. | Social workers--United States.
Classification: DDC 362.860973--dc23

Printed in Singapore

To Thomas, for everything;
and to Ashley, Sam and Maximus, three keys to my heart.

This book was written in honor of the veterans who have
graced my life. Thank you for letting me be of service.

CONTENTS

PROLOGUE

March 2003. Six months earlier, I had begun my tour of duty at the West Los Angeles Department of Veterans Affairs. I was a social worker in a small, residential program providing drug and alcohol treatment. The guys filed in from chow hall, seating themselves for "group."

During lunch, a TV mounted on a tall stand had been wheeled into the center of the circle.

The day before, American troops had invaded Iraq. The next day, we gathered around CNN images of young troops marching into war and members of the George W. Bush Cabinet explaining why. In the weeks to come, veterans would speak ruefully about those early days of war: "What the fuck is that for? Why're we going in again? People're gonna die. We [Americans] don't learn."

On this day, though, they were silent. No one wanted to miss this moment in history. Like Operation Desert Storm, we figured, it would be over in about a week.

On June 30, 2017—fourteen-and-a-half years later—I left the Department of Veterans Affairs, but the Iraq War, in some variation or other, was still going on.

INTRODUCTION

I never intended to work with veterans.

I had never met one, in fact; or so I thought. My father served in World War II, but he was not my idea of a veteran. At five feet two inches tall, Sam was no warrior. More brains than brawn, he lacked all aptitude for mechanics and had no taste for physical aggression. But he was a typing whiz, so throughout his tour of duty he was stationed behind a 1940s Remington typewriter. Better for the country and for him.

The other soldiers in my life were actors. A TV child actress of the sixties, my wide-eyed urchin look put me on the frontlines of four episodes of the hit 1960s World War II TV series, "Combat!" In numerous scenes, the late Vic Morrow shielded me from imaginary bomb blasts (silence on the set!) and flying pieces of glass (plastic). I will always remember the acrid smell of artificial smoke and the rush of testosterone from this all-male cast, but I was too young to fully appreciate it and reciprocate.

I was in high school and college during the Vietnam War. Not a single guy I hung out with served. They knew the deal: Stay in school, dodge the draft. Some pleaded economic or financial "hardship." Together, we marched against the Vietnam War and, shamefully, against its warriors. While a student in the 1970s at UC Berkeley, ROTC (the Reserve Officers' Training Corps) was shunned.

I was, then, an odd mix: part Hollywood, part Red Diaper baby. After the Service, during the rise of McCarthyism, my father was blacklisted. He lost his job at City College of New York and moved to LA to find work. He did, as a research librarian at UCLA—and my parents found work for me, too, on TV. Thus, I was weaned on Lenin, Marx, Rod Serling and Alfred Hitchcock.

I guess it was easier to take the kid out of Hollywood, and Hollywood out of the kid, than the left-leaning liberalism out of the daughter of the blacklisted Red. In 2000, I decided to enter the field of social work, and two years later graduated with a Master's degree from the UCLA School of Public Policy/Social Work. A "temp" agency placed me at the VA. There, I earned the mandatory 3200 hours of on-the-job clinical supervision and passed the massive two-part California State licensing exam in 2005. Homeless? Drug addicts? The chronically mentally ill? I hadn't a clue. But I wanted a job, and the VA was close to where I lived.

Friends thought I would find the work there too frustrating, too gritty, too demoralizing. Or, as I was once asked by my friend Dwayne Hickman, best known as 1960s TV icon Dobie Gillis, "Isn't that depressing?" Well, isn't Hollywood? With all the lies? Said he: "You bet!"

It was precisely this gritty realism that attracted me. No artifice. No trick angles. No pretending. I was in the trenches, and I loved it.

This is the sentiment I hope to convey here. I have no desire to indict this leviathan of a government institution; everyone knows the VA is a bureaucratic mess. What people don't know, perhaps, is the underlying story: the zany passion and persistence of social workers serving veterans; the crushing pain but astounding resilience of veterans who come to them for help; and the moments when all the stars are aligned, the supply meets the demand, and something good—maybe even great—comes of it.

I served veterans of many wars and "conflicts": Vietnam; Operation Desert Storm (the Persian Gulf War); Operation Iraqi Freedom; Operation Enduring Freedom (Afghanistan); the Korean War; Somalia; Kuwait; and Yemen. They came in all colors and stripes: Caucasian. African American. Hispanic. Asian. Geographically, almost all of these death traps were in Asia.

In my fourteen-and-a-half years there, I worked with many dedicated people who continue, today, to fight against horrific odds (inadequate funding and staffing, danger in the workplace, shifting political winds and policies). This is the story I want to tell.

What follows is my memory of life as a social worker on the frontlines of the Department of Veterans Affairs.

Chapter One

THE LITTLE SHOP OF HORRORS
2002–2003

The Veterans Health Administration, America's largest integrated healthcare system, consists of 1,250 healthcare facilities—including 172 medical centers and 1,069 outpatient sites of care operating clinics, hospitals, centers for community living and readjustment counseling services. I was once part of that system.

Each year, the VA nationwide serves 9 million enrolled veterans.

The West LA campus is the largest VA facility in the U.S. Stretching across 400 acres, it is like one country with two cultures, divided by Wilshire Boulevard, one of the principal east-west arterial roads in Los Angeles.

To the north is the "mental health side," where veterans are treated for disorders such as schizophrenia, severe depression, post-traumatic stress disorder and addiction. The buildings are old, if not crumbling. My placement there was the Domiciliary, which started as an old soldiers' home in the 1930s but evolved into a residential treatment program, or holding cell, for homeless veterans.

To the south is the Medical Center, a six-floor modern monolith which provides traditional inpatient and outpatient care as well as an array of specialty services, such as the poly-trauma clinic, for veterans with traumatic brain injury (TBI), one of the signature marks of our wars in Afghanistan and Iraq; and the Women's Clinic.

Overall, the West LA VA campus looks like a university in default—a cache of concrete and stucco buildings tucked into Brentwood, a swanky spot on LA's affluent West Side. The main neighborhood drag is San Vicente, a broad, busy boulevard that virtually glitters with chic clothing boutiques, coffee boutiques, workout establishments (Soul Cycle, Orange Theory) and trendy cafes. Once, after lunching at the famed San Vicente Tavern restaurant (built upon the ruins of a Hamburger Hamlet), President Obama waved to the troops across the street.

This is not Beverly Hills, 90210. This is Brentwood, 90409.

Newbie

I was a novice, and everyone could tell. I'd seen Hollywood, Berkeley, New York and LA. I'd accompanied my husband on journalistic jaunts across Southeast Asia. But I'd never seen the Veterans Health Administration. The parking lot, an asphalt square encircled by weeds, was a showcase of bumper and window stickers: Proud Marine. Khe Sanh 1964. U.S. Army. MIA. POW. Airborne, followed by a line of numbers. None of it made sense.

The cars themselves told tales, but it took me a year or so to decipher them. There were abandoned jalopies jacked up on wooden planks, like lifeless whales speared and washed ashore. There were cars and trucks permanently parked, no driver in sight and not a wheel moved for days and months. These were signs that the owner had died, was in jail, or had no money for gas or professional repairs. By contrast, there were sleek, new models (green Jaguars, gold Cadillacs) that meant the owner had come into a trove of government money, and spent it at once.

That first day, I was to report to the Opiate Treatment Program (known as OTP), at 7:00 a.m. The first thing within view was a pair of cop cars with flashing lights parked halfway up the lawn, just before the entrance. Inside the building the two cops, each grasping an arm of a pale, skinny, disheveled guy in handcuffs, escorted him down the long hall to their car outside. Someone on the sidelines shouted, "How ya doin', man?" Hands cuffed behind his back, he attempted a small shrug. It was the first time I saw a man up close in cuffs.

The Opiate Treatment Program, as its name suggests, helps veterans detox from heroin or prescription opiates (Vicodin, Norco, Oxycodone). There, methadone (a prescribed opiate) is dispensed to ease symptoms of heroin withdrawal (joint aches, stomach pains). Some are actually on methadone maintenance—those whose risk for relapse is so high, and their addiction so severe, they might die if detoxed from both heroin and methadone. Instead, they take a daily dose of liquid methadone, dispensed at the clinic (later on there might be "take-homes"), and do so sometimes for years, even decades, while leading productive lives. (Today there are newer, more preferred medications, such as buprenorphine, otherwise known as suboxone). Many of these men (and a few women) had addiction problems prior to their military service that intensified during those years. Others, particularly the younger set, developed substance abuse problems as a result of mental health disorders, such as post-traumatic stress disorder (PTSD), incurred during their periods of service.

That first day in September, 2003, and every day thereafter for six months, I walked through the clinic door and whisked by a line of guys waiting for their methadone hand-outs. Every day, it was the same. One by one, in smooth but rapid succession, each veteran would step up to the window; reach through the small opening to retrieve a Dixie cup filled with methadone; carry it to his lips; toss his head back; and swallow, in one gulp. The pharmacist's face, visible through the window, looked solemn and grim—like a TV actor playing a forensic scientist on "Law & Order." He alone was allowed entry into this treasure trove of opiates, which added to its mystery and allure. How I wanted, sometimes, to line up for a dose—just once! They say if you've never done heroin or methadone, a tiny hit of this liquid opiate will make you high.

My job at OTP was to conduct "biopsychosocial assessments." These are the lifeblood of the VA—formatted questionnaires used to establish a patient's medical, psychological, and social history. For me, they were easy to do. I had authored two books, written many magazine stories, and held a Master's degree in journalism (in addition to social work). I was a speed demon at typing. But as a newcomer to the addiction field, there were some odd job-specific skills to learn. For example: How to conduct an interview while the subject is doubled over in abdominal pain because he's withdrawing from heroin. How to refrain from offering a tissue to a patient with a runny nose (he isn't crying or having an allergy attack; he's withdrawing). How to ask a former warrior if drugs made him impotent or killed his libido. My go-to formulation was, "Are you heterosexual?" (If "yes," we moved along unless he commented further.) My favorite response, from a Vietnam vet who pounded the wall with his fist: "Me?? Rock hard!"

Proceed with Caution

This was my first hour of the day. Then I would move to the program next door, known as RTC (Recovery Treatment Center). That first day, walking down the long, dark hall, I felt profound disappointment. So quiet! So calm! Where were the patients and staff!? Sure, it was a small program, but was this the wrong place?

Then the silence was broken. I heard a woman shouting: "You lousy, pudgy loser! You used to get girls but they don't want you now! You dragged your whole family in with you, crying, and you don't even care!"—in a mental health care/substance abuse treatment facility??

I continued down the hallway, now with dread, until it ended in a set of double doors shut tight. An oddly narrow, vertical window was built into each door. I soon learned that all of the office doors had these windows, everywhere at the VA, and that they served a dual purpose: (1) to ensure privacy; and (2) to guarantee that, in the event of patient violence, passersby looking in could come to the rescue. This harkened back to that first day of graduate school, when social work professors urged against wearing tight skirts and high heels, which could hamper fast getaways.

The doors cracked open, and for a moment the profanity-laced screams grew louder, then stopped. This was the "day room," a large, gymnasium-like space with very little furniture and big voices echoing throughout, thanks to great acoustics. A dozen men seated in a semi-circle stared back at me. (Months later, they laughed at how I looked—"Like a deer caught in the headlights.") Well, they were right. The closest I'd come to guys like these were black-and-white photos, on the walls of my parents' post office, marked "WANTED." How I loved to stare at them! (My first fascination with Bad Boys.)

The back of a woman was facing me, as she was turned away, staring hard at the guys—obviously the group facilitator. This was Dr. Isobel Dalali, lovingly called "Dr. D," in one of her renowned group therapy sessions. She was an unlikely program boss: age seventy at least, with a gorgeous face slathered in pancake make-up, eyes ringed by thick black liquid liner, peroxided hair slicked into a severely tight bun, and a leopard-print scarf draped around her neck. She turned and waved me in without a word. A former model (of hats and gloves—too short for the runway), Dr. D held a PhD in psychology from UCLA. But it was years before her move to LA, at the University of Minnesota, that she was inspired by her mentor, famed behavioral scientist B.F. Skinner, to someday launch RTC, one of the first residential substance abuse treatment and rehabilitation programs on the West LA VA campus. Throughout thirty years of government service, she had become a legend: a diminutive dynamo with a big mind, a big mouth, and a big heart; a career government worker with true star power; a woman born into wealth who chose to work with the hardest, toughest, most recalcitrant and recidivist men at the VA… and who was able to make them cry. To some administrators, she was a liability. To some veterans, a savior. To many, the pain of her harsh ways was worth the price of admission to a sober future.

Attack Therapy

If you came of age in the sixties, you have heard of Synanon, one of America's first community drug treatment programs. It touted an alternative lifestyle as well as instruction on how to live drug-free (e.g., drop out of mainstream society, tune in to the counterculture). Founded in 1958, the core Synanon belief was that in order to become substance-free one must break free of the past; that every addict hides behind a brick wall of defensiveness and denial; and that the wall must be torn down, using blunt instruments. Thus, the "Synanon Game" was born, a therapeutic technique in which a patient sits in the center of a circle of peers who offer sharp criticism, even attacks, so as to tear down, then rebuild his character. This method was billed as truth-telling.

Twenty years later, the program began to decline. In 1978, its founder, Charles E. Dederich, was arrested for drunk driving. Then he pleaded no contest to charges of conspiracy to commit murder (by helping place a four-foot rattlesnake, minus its rattles, in the mailbox of a lawyer who had been litigating against Synanon). Dederich was also arrested for an alleged stock fraud scheme. In 1991, the program finally collapsed under the weight of controversies and criminal charges, including acts of violence (beating juveniles referred there by the California courts) and corruption (the Internal Revenue Service sued for $17 million in back taxes, whereby all Synanon property was confiscated and sold).

The Recovery Treatment Center was highly derivative of Synanon. Also known as "attack therapy," this interrogative style suited some vets, especially those with long histories of relapse and long rap sheets to match. RTC was their last resort; one more mess-up would lead to death, jail or both. Accordingly, the program capitalized on tough love and strict discipline, and had many prohibitions, such as: No talking to anyone not in the program. No venturing outside the VA gates alone, or without permission. No talking to women. No talking back to authority. And more. There were multiple mandates: Walk in group formation. Sit up straight. Make your bed, military-style (so that a coin can be bounced off the corners). Follow all directions, unquestioningly.

To achieve compliance, she used techniques to foster humiliation: Walk like a duck. Sit in the corner on a stool, wearing a dunce cap (I only heard about these—by the time I got there, she'd grown softer, with commands like: Sit on the group sidelines. Write the same apologetic statement 100 times). It all seemed unduly harsh, maybe even abusive; but in 2003, there were few widely used and accepted treatment alternatives. Alcoholics Anonymous was already more than fifty years old, and in 1958 alcoholism had been labeled by the American Medical Association a "brain disease." But the stigma of weak moral character, rather than genetic and environmental influences, lived on. I still remember my parents' reaction when a distant cousin, a hard-luck, would-be actress-model ten years older than I, mailed notices of her upcoming appearance in a play performed at Synanon. The enlightened Marxist and his dedicated wife snickered—and did not see the play.

Dr. D was brilliant. She could take the most seemingly trivial behavioral detail—leaving a light on, forgetting to make the bed—and concoct it into a tale of impending relapse. For example: Ken R failed to turn off the lights in his room. "Why?" she said, hectoring him in group until he admitted his wrong. He explained that he "lost focus" when his wife called, begging him to quit programming and come home. If you were sloppy enough to forget the rules, she said, if you didn't know right from wrong, or didn't care which was which, you were likely to slip into relapse mode and wind up right back where you started… or dead.

For a long time, I thought this was madness, but after a few months I came to understand her technique. Imagine finding yourself parked in the driveway at home. You're there! You barely remember driving, and yet you didn't run lights or cause a crash. You were subliminally aware—so sure of the rules, so used to following them for so long—that safe driving protocol was embedded in your brain. Now apply this line of thinking to addiction: You practice sober behaviors so many times, so often, that you don't have to think about saying "no" to the drink or the drug. Just as your knee bounces back when the doctor tests your reflexes, so does the sober mind.

The end justified the means. No practice was considered too harsh if it led to sobriety. There were many confrontational groups. One was called "logging." All day every day, patients were mandated to observe others' behaviors, note "slips" or rule violations, and record them in the big, thick, odious "log book." Then in group, each veteran who wrote a citation had to read it aloud to the accused, in an odd kind of spectator sport, with patients like ringside spectators to a gladiatorial contest. Logging was supposedly aimed at helping vets abandon bad habits cultivated on the street and in prison—"snitching" was transformed into truthfulness.

Such was Dr. D's version of Skinner's radical behaviorism, based on the core belief that behavior is a consequence of environment and reinforcement. Accordingly, she believed that a changed environment would induce and reinforce behavioral change. But did that changed environment justify maintaining a police state?

For less stable veterans, her extreme punitive style could be traumatic. When you throw a vase to the floor, will it shatter into tiny fragments? Or can it be pieced back as a whole? You could never tell, in advance. Suddenly, a veteran might begin to wither under verbal siege—neck veins bulging, eyes misting, knees bobbing from nerves. Suddenly he would rise from his chair, rip his cardboard name tag to shreds, and walk off, never to return.

John C was one such case. The trouble began when he cut a corner of the crosswalk and fell out of formation. The men had been marching to a Thursday night meeting of AA, as they did every week, three miles down San Vicente Boulevard to the Brentwood Presbyterian Church. The meetings were one of the high points of each week. There would be lots of women with high-end cars, high fashion clothes and breast implants that bounced like basketballs when they sobbed. The vets dubbed it "Silicone Valley."

"What were you thinking?" Dr. D roared when John's violation was reported in group. "What took away your attention?" Withering under her prosecution, John confessed: It was the sight of a woman's "hot, tight ass." He admitted to "reckless eyeballing"—this was VA-speak for the way men leer at women as sex objects. And so, Dr. D devised a punishment befitting the crime: John was to walk inside the therapy circle, stop closely before each seated individual (staff too) and wait for each to guess whether he placed his genitals to the left or the right of his zipper. Her point, obviously, was: See how it feels to be sexually humiliated and harassed!

This was one of the rare moments I was truly shocked. What would people outside the program say if they found out? Or social work professors? Or family? I panicked, and when John got to me, I turned my head aside, refusing to look. He proceeded to the next person and went on until completing the round.

The next morning, Dr. D confronted me: "You're a prude! So prissy!" I did not object. I did not say that this former Berkeley girl had seen a crotch or two—or more. I did not say that it was ethical judgment, rather than squeamishness, which made me look away. I let her vent. She was *not* a force to be reckoned with—not at age seventy, after decades of clinical practice.

A few days later, John C left the program. A year or two after that, we met up, by chance, in the hospital cafeteria, where he was working as a food server. The past did not come up, but he looked like he was doing well.

I confess: At other times, I was complicit in the humiliation. Could I have objected more, and sooner? Sure. But I was new to the field. For all my life experience, it would take time to develop a sound therapeutic style and learn to balance program rules with humaneness.

Attack therapy is pretty much maligned now. RTC was dissolved just a few years after Dr. Dalali's death in 2012. Serious efforts have been made to ensure more appropriate, careful referrals that better suit prospective patients' needs. In 2017 the NIAAA (National Institute on Alcohol Abuse and Alcoholism), for example, launched its "Alcohol Treatment Navigator," a series of questions and quality indicators that would, effectively, help people steer clear of such treatment protocols. Even the mass media caught on. In June of 2018, *The Washington Post*, writing about the Alcohol Treatment Navigator, referred to how "in low quality treatment programs, individual and group counseling is composed largely of unstructured, unproductive chat or *aggressive confrontations designed to shame patients.* Fortunately, there are structured, evidenced-based psychotherapies with higher levels of effectiveness." Down with tough love!

This is a good thing, and it's global. In 2001—just before I started at the VA—therapists from twelve treatment centers in Thailand jetted off to Santa Monica, California, then headquarters of the Matrix Institute for substance abuse recovery, to get state-of-the-art training. The country's drug epidemic had been worsening. Methamphetamine had replaced heroin as the drug of choice. It was time for a new approach.

Fourteen years later, the trend continued. In February 2015, a report of the *International Journal of Drug Policy* reported that: "Over the last three decades in response to a rise in substance use in the region, many countries in East and Southeast Asia responded by establishing laws and policies that allowed for compulsory detention in the name of treatment for people who use drugs. These centers have recently come under international scrutiny with a call for their closure in a Joint Statement from United Nations entities in March 2012." It highlighted that "A change to an evidence-based approach is taking place in several countries in Asia."

Other treatment trends today are traditional Eastern practices aimed at stress-relief: meditation, yoga, tai-chi. Veterans love tai-chi. Not so much yoga—too girlish!—but tai-chi is both calming... and a martial art.

Cease and Desist

Things were less combative in "Goals and Directions." This was a group focused on public speaking skills—kind of like Toastmasters, but for veterans. Dr. D assigned me to facilitate. It was a good fit. A former child actress, I knew a few things about speaking clearly and projecting personality.

Each morning I guided the guys through their individual routine: step up to the dayroom podium; state your name and drug of choice; then state your goal for the day (being honest, not using drugs or alcohol, making amends). I prodded them to speak clearly and with conviction, but they had a tough time. Public speaking takes confidence, which most of them lacked due to years of drug abuse, childhood abuse, abandonment and violence. But they tried, admirably, and took enormous pride in their progress. Lloyd, a fifty-six-year-old crack addict, actually cried when he completed the program. "You don't know what it meant to me to be able to speak like that!" he said. "I could never do it in school." It is a common adage that addicts cease to develop emotionally, psychologically and socially from the moment they start abusing drugs. This is because, rather than learning from life experience, they hide behind a high. The joy of emerging into the light, center-stage and sober, thrilled both them and me.

Overall, this RTC stint was a fabulous foray into social work. Every day, a rush of uncensored, unadulterated emotions coursed through my veins: Guilt. Shame. Anger. Desperation. Sincerity. Fellowship. Healing. Empathy. Triumph. It was life on the edge, exhausting and exhilarating. Like a soldier in combat, I was addicted to the high.

Lessons Learned

What I learned those first six months stayed with me for the next fourteen-and-a-half years.

I learned that to feel complacent could be dangerous, if not fatal. The men of RTC were, if anything, overly compliant. They emptied trash cans. They cleaned sinks. And they never complained. Criminals? These guys? Said a supervising social worker: "You're seeing them clean!" He reminded me that drug abuse leads to crime, and that these sweet men were capable of great violence in their desperation for drugs. Then when he saw my social work license, framed and propped on top of my desk, he grabbed it: "Are you crazy? Don't display your home address! Do you want to lose your furniture—or your life?"

I learned to take no credit for patients' successes or failures. I learned that at best I could be their guide, but the hard work of getting sober was on them. And I learned never to predict outcomes. One day I might enjoy a great therapeutic rapport with a patient, only to learn the next morning that an hour or two later he had gotten drunk and taken off. As they say in Alanon, the AA sister program for friends and families of alcoholics: "You didn't cause it; you can't control it; and you can't cure it." You can only try to help.

I learned, up close and personal, that relapse is part of recovery. Very few patients stay clean on their first try. It could take months, years, and innumerable programs to, as the saying goes, "hit rock bottom." I learned to think that he who relapses after twenty years is: (1) someone who enjoyed considerable success, and (2) someone currently in trouble. I learned, too, never to convey disappointment or disapproval to someone struggling with addiction; it would further discourage the patient by lowering his self-esteem.

I learned that my veteran patients were not my friends. I learned to maintain boundaries, and that while self-disclosure serves a therapeutic purpose—you reveal a little, the patient tells a lot—it can morph into "too much of a good thing." Share an intimacy, like a fight with your spouse, and a veteran will make good use of it, playing mind games and manipulating you for personal gain.

I learned not to add too many personal touches to my office. Lewis, a middle-aged truck driver with diagnoses of crack abuse and bipolar disorder, seemed oddly fidgety his first time in my office. "I used to kill cats," he said. "I would drown them sometimes in the bathtub and watch them die. It gave me a sense of power, I guess." Surrounded by my cat mugs, cat calendar, and Asian art works featuring cats, Lewis was unnerved. He probably felt ashamed (amazing that he confessed his crimes to an obvious lover of fabulous felines!). Nevertheless, we still had to work together, which was hard for us both. I got rid of every object and artwork in feline form.

I also learned some very important VA lingo, including:

- *normie*: someone who doesn't ruin their lives by abusing alcohol or drugs. Someone who has a car, a job, and a mortgage. Me. You.

- *hoochie mama*: a hooker. A woman who is NOT a normie. She wears sky-high stilettos and micro-minis.

- *classy woman*: opposite of the above. A woman who dresses like a professional, gets manicures, and never, ever sits like a "crack whore," legs wide open to invite men in.

- *drug of choice* or *DOC*: whichever mind-altering substance the patient loves most; therefore, the one that does him greatest harm, whether crack, alcohol, heroin… whatever. Many patients abuse multiple drugs simultaneously (crack for the excitation, alcohol to calm down; marijuana for the calm, meth to perk up). Others have no preference. Ask, "What's your drug of choice?" and they say, "What you got?"

- *three hots and a cot*: three warm meals and a bed to sleep in, which constitutes a homeless person's bottom-line. Sometimes this phrase is used disparagingly, to describe the veteran who doesn't give a hoot about recovery and "just" wants a hand-out.

- *stinkin' thinkin'*: disturbed, unhealthful, circuitous cognitive patterns unique to addicts and alcoholics, usually resulting in relapse. For example: "I've already blown my sobriety, so why stop now?" "I can quit. I've done it many times." "I only binge on weekends." These phrases travel, even to the Betty Ford Center.

In 2005, Dr. Dalali was given a Congressional Medal in honor of thirty years of VA service. A year later, she retired from the VA. Granted emeritus status, she continued to teach one or two groups a week until 2012, when she died of pancreatic cancer while working on her memoirs. This woman, a pioneer in the recovery field, remained dedicated to the cause to the end. For that, I admired her.

End of an Era: The Funeral of Dr. D

I squinted on the way to the chapel. It was an exceptionally sunny, bright, crisp December day. The sun's glare cast an almost psychedelic sheen on the manicured expanse of emerald lawn. Guys huddled on the chapel steps, hugging and asking, "Are we gonna make it?"

I felt sorry for them. They had lost their Higher Power. Their Divine Leader. Their Chairman Mao and Ho Chi Minh.

Suited up and sober, they filed down the aisle to their seats, a few high-fiving me while passing by.

The back pews were Relapse Row. Here sat the gaunt, the unshaven, and the obviously unwell. They stared at the floor and did not mingle. I knew why, of course. Many a vet boasts about never going to church drunk or high. So they skip church. But as this was a special, one-time event, they came as they were.

As I stood by my seat before the ceremony started, someone tapped my shoulder. It was a middle-aged white guy in a suit. I didn't recognize him, until he said his name. His full name. Then I remembered him: Ron R, the lone Jewish vet I had encountered at RTC—one of the very few Jewish veterans anywhere at the VA, in fact. Ten years earlier, in group, he had talked about stealing his parents' TV, pushing it in a shopping cart to a pawn shop and selling it for drug money. The vets listened and laughed. "We've all been there," one explained. "It's a kind of nervous laugh." Then another voice rang out: "At least he didn't take his kids' Christmas presents from under the tree!"

Ron R said he was doing well. He had the looks and bearing to match. He claimed to be ten years sober. He had a job and a wife. When he introduced us, she smiled, eyes cast downward, a silent worshiper in the recovery world. Said Ron R, with deep intensity in his voice and eyes, "I have a life. And I owe it all to Dr. D."

Lift-Off

After six months as a contract worker, I accepted an offer to become a full-time VA staff social worker. My new placement would be the Domiciliary, building 217. Known as "the Dom," this was actually a two-building (217 and 214), 280-bed residential program for veterans who were homeless, addicted to drugs and alcohol, and chronically mentally ill.

I had misgivings about leaving RTC. I'd grown attached to the small, dysfunctional, family-style program. It was at once claustrophobic and protective. By contrast, the Domiciliary was the hub of the VA, with spokes radiating to every program, clinic and ward on campus. But the VA wheel moves slowly, in circles, over a time-worn, rutted road. From the start, I feared being crushed beneath its bureaucratic weight.

I'd heard stories about the dangers that lurked beyond, like the one about the ultra-confident psychologist who insisted she could singlehandedly manage a wildly erratic veteran with an extensive history of violence. One day, during a one-on-one closed-door session, the patient beat her up. She survived, and even stayed on at the VA, but transferred to the women's clinic.

In addition, I didn't want to leave the field of substance abuse.

My RTC supervisor, a young upstart social worker destined to go on to bigger and better things at other VAs across the country, set me straight with this simple proviso: Where there is homelessness, there is substance abuse. Think about it: Did homelessness lead to mental illness and drug abuse? Or did drug abuse lead to homelessness? Wherever it starts, what follows is a downward spiral.

"You'll see plenty of drugs there," he said, "just like everywhere else at the VA."

You can say that again.

Chapter Two

THE GREAT WALL OF THE VA
2003–2007, THE "W" YEARS

The day after his Domiciliary admission, Trevor came to me with an urgent request: He had to get to a cash machine, fast, so could I waive his thirty-day restriction to VA grounds? At the Recovery Treatment Center, such a request would have been unthinkable; but the Domiciliary was a much looser, more evolved, vet-friendly program. Requests like this were made all the time, especially by veteran newbies. Typically, they would say, "I have to take care of business." Ask for more information, and you'd get: "Business!" That's all.

Trevor had just come off the street. I knew nothing about him, so I wasn't going to waive the rule. That would invite liability—suppose he kills himself? Or someone else? Or dies of an overdose, robs a bank, steals a car or a child? Healthy paranoia makes for sound clinical judgment.

Trevor could tell my answer was "no." Exasperated, he clapped both hands to his head, then lowered his head to his lap and actually whimpered.

In a therapy group the next morning, however, Trevor seemed calm. Our topic of discussion that day was the fine line between failure and success. Hasn't everyone been fired at least once, I asked? All hands were raised—except Trevor's. He had never been fired, he explained—because he had never been hired: "I've never had a job." He said it with a straight face, and no one laughed. How could this be?

This purportedly "fresh start" in rehab actually marked his *thirty-third* admission to a treatment program. Of course he had never worked! He had been in treatment for cocaine addiction virtually his entire adult civilian life. As he put it, "I'm good at living in programs, but I'm bad when I leave." Patients like this are dubbed "institutionalized"—unable to cope independently in the adult world. Needing guidance all the time. Crippled by too much "help."

Trevor entered the Navy at age eighteen, but his drug problems began in his early teens. Joining the military didn't help. Drugs and alcohol provided a failsafe way to ease tensions and fit in with the guys. As a hearty post-adolescent, he could withstand the adverse effects of all those poisons he ingested. Now in his fifties, things had changed.

Not surprisingly, Trevor had mastered the recovery world. Every day he wore a plain white tee-shirt and jeans devoid of creases or stains—he had several sets, which he ironed daily in the residents' laundry room. He enjoyed the routine. What's more, he was fantastic in groups—truthful, eloquent, and polished. His voice purred like a high-end car, while his eyes glistened with excitement as he spoke—even when, for the thirty-third time, he confessed to leaving the wedding party, his wife in her bridal gown, to get high.

Sometimes I wondered: Is this guy slick? Is he for real? Am I being played? In fact, this lifetime patient was so polished and knowledgeable that I actually wound up using him as a co-counselor, assisting me with groups, even running them himself when we were short-staffed. This is called "peer counseling." Now a widely accepted practice, "student" teachers help bridge the socioeconomic gap between Us and Them.

What a pro! Trevor knew just how to look animated and interested in others' stories (because he truly was), how to sit patiently through each veteran's so-called confessional talk, or "share," and how to slip in a quick "thank you" at each story's end. I once remarked that I'd love to hire him. Smiling, he reminded me that he lacked one central job qualification: "I don't have a year's sobriety." Oh, yeah. I forgot about that.

In the Trenches

Having survived boot camp, I considered myself battle-ready.

Wrong. I could not have anticipated what was to come: Overdoses. Patient deaths. Patient threats. Staff threats. Assaults. "Clean" urine for sale to bypass routine drug tests. Bedbugs. Norovirus. Sodas stolen from the community refrigerator. Room inspections. Contraband. Drug-sniffing dogs. Butcher knives stashed inside lockers, under beds, in drawers.

To be fair, there were some great things, too: Caring staff. Vets helping vets. Vets getting clean. Deep therapeutic ties. Reconciled marriages. New jobs. Enhanced self-esteem. Fellowship. Sustained sobriety.

Still, it was boot camp all over again.

The Domiciliary Residential Rehabilitation and Treatment Program, or DRRTP

The "Dom," as it was called by both patients and staff, refers to two buildings on opposite ends of an asphalt quad lined by trees and grass. This was a favored gathering spot for veterans. Seated side by side on benches, they smoked (when no staffer was looking), talked, or simply stared ahead, perhaps envisioning some kind of future. Smoking areas that looked like bus stops were located inconveniently far from this activity hub.

The Dom maintained a full-time, in-house staff of clinicians, mostly psychologists and social workers, whose chief goal was to keep the mental peace and help veterans find permanent housing in LA. When I started in 2003, there was no mental health or substance abuse programming. For actual treatment, residents were farmed out to VA clinics on West LA grounds, like DDTP (the Dual Diagnosis Treatment Program, for veterans with schizophrenia), MHC (the Mental Health Clinic, for those with non-psychotic, non-hallucinatory mental health disorders), ATC (the Addiction Treatment Clinic, for vets needing alcohol and substance abuse treatment), and POST (outpatient treatment for those diagnosed with PTSD). Every day, Dom patients, some pushing wheelchairs and walkers, made their way a half-mile north, under the freeway bridge, for appointments at the south side medical center. Some caught the VA shuttle bus.

In 2003, there were just three social workers (including me) serving 280 men. There were also two MDs, two psychologists, no psychiatrist, and no security guards. There were phantom employees—people whose names and job titles appeared on floor directories, office doors, flow charts... but were never at work. Some took stress leave, which was easy to get. LA has lots of swanky doctors who once "did time," meaning residency, at the VA. They could feel their patients' pain and did not hesitate to write leave requests for psychological and emotional relief. Other absences were due to: medical or mental health disability claims; workmen's comp claims; and ongoing litigation regarding abuse of power, sexual harassment, racism, and any form of discrimination known to man, or woman (there were just a few then). Some of these workers were in fact on VA grounds, although not at the Dom—they had been "detailed" (military-speak for reassigned) to other clinics. Adjudication could take weeks, months, even years, but their jobs remained open and unfilled, since they had neither been fired nor quit. The left-behind, non-litigious had to cover their work, until those employees, too, took stress leave. What a waste of time and resources! In the end, nearly all returned to their original posts.

Finally, there were "the redeployed"—employees who were also veterans, sent back to Afghanistan and Iraq, sometimes for a year or more. But while serving overseas, their names remained on the VA flowchart and they were counted as current employees. By listing names of people in absentia, administrators made the program look decently staffed—on paper. And at the VA, there is no shortage of paper, or people poring over it.

In the interim, social workers covered for them all. Who else?

Class Warfare

The Domiciliary, like all of the VA, was entirely and intensely political, and politically correct, at all levels and in ways I could not have imagined, affecting every vein, artery and organ of its being.

It was overly inclusive. The place pretended to be a color-blind, egalitarian, classless, multidisciplinary mecca. In a way, for the patients this was true. They were all together in the VA mess. All races. All kinds. All bands of brothers. Roy Nishikori, a fifty-seven-year-old Japanese-American former Marine, was nicknamed "Chinaman." He didn't mind. A crack addict with bipolar disorder, Roy was happy to please his buddies by putting his upbeat, hyperactive bipolar mood swings to good use. He ordered pizzas for the Super Bowl and extra patient pillows. Roy's comrades didn't even care that he was gay. And wore a man bun.

Staff was less open-minded. In practice, there were two warring Dom factions: Mine, made up of the trained clinical staff (social workers, psychologists, MDs, nurses, dieticians); and the paraprofessionals, trained in the school of hard knocks of their own recovery (peer support technicians, certified addiction therapists, Domiciliary Assistants who manned the plant and managed the rooms, the daily admissions, the bed checks—kind of like wardens, which is how, I'm pretty sure, they frequently felt). We clinicians had academic credentials; they had "street cred." We advocated the positivism of "patient-centered" care, empathic listening and motivational interviewing; the paraprofessional "Dom Assistants," as they were called, favored the negative reinforcement of "tough love," confrontational therapy, and punitive actions for bad behaviors.

Typical exchanges went like this:

"What do you know about addiction? You've never been homeless!"

"That's true, but I have the degree and my license is on the line."

"All you know is books! You look down on me because I don't have 'that piece of paper'!" (Education counts against you? That's a new one!)

"Wrong. I value your input, but in the end, I have to do what I think is right."

Patients were confused. Directions came from two staff armies issuing opposite commands. For example: A DA (Dom Assistant) working overnight (they were the only paraprofessionals forced to work the dreaded 12:00 p.m. to 8:00 a.m. shift) might be faced with an unruly and uncooperative resident—someone ranting under the influence of alcohol and drugs, let's say, or punching walls, if not other patients. The Dom Assistant might in turn blow up and respond by issuing immediate discharge orders to the troublesome vet: "You're outta here, now! Pack your bags!" With that, the vet would be forced back to the streets, homeless, in the middle of the night. Alternatively, the Dom Assistant might say, with the appearance of great certainty and authority, "You will be discharged tomorrow! Meet with your clinical treatment team in the morning!"

Then my buddies and I—we clinicians, perceived to be the privileged elite—would arrive at work following a good night's sleep and remand the DA's orders: "He can't do that! This isn't a prison! This has to be a clinical decision!" To which the DA might fight back: "You don't know what the guy's like when you're not here. He needs to pay a price! We need to put him out, now!"

Rage would sweep up the chain of command, to the two at the top. Number one was my boss, the Chief of the Domiciliary and supervisor of clinical operations. She was a tall, slender, African American woman, elegant in manner and appearance, a cross dangling from a gold chain around her neck, beautifully but conservatively dressed (high necklines and long skirts). Her name was Zina, but we called her "the Chief." Second in command: the Assistant Chief (boss of the Dom Assistants and other paraprofessionals), a female sergeant, also African American, who barked orders in military jargon but was called Jean or Ms. Carter.

They were no great match. Battle lines drawn, both protected their troops. Who would surrender? Sometimes, VA higher-ups in D.C. were called in to settle the score. Mind you, wounded warriors wandering the streets make for bad politics and bad headlines, so top brass usually sided with the clinicians. The job got easier, then, when a resurgence of "patient dumping" onto the streets became widespread news. Hotshots at the national level forbade any Domiciliary discharge that wasn't "bulletproof"—meaning one that included: an address, an available bed as verified by staff at that address, a means of transportation to get there, and copious documentation of it all. At the very least.

Unfortunately, patient dumping, which started in the 1960s with the deinstitutionalization of the mentally ill, continues today. Why would hospitals discharge patients without safe discharge plans? Because there are no good, viable housing options; because sometimes patients won't accept available options ("Don't send me there! It's not safe!"—they had a point); or because doctors want these men and women out of the hospital, "Tonight!" Then, the social worker's options are to: (1) advocate for the patient's rights; (2) come up with a perfect plan executed on very short notice; or (3) cave and send the patient to a shelter or even the street, praying that he finds safety.

In January 2018, in fact, a woman diagnosed with schizophrenia and autism was discharged by the University of Maryland
Medical Center to the streets (in her hospital gown!). The hospital
CEO apologized to the patient, called it an "isolated incident" and
vowed to investigate further as well as review its discharge policies.

What's a social worker to do? Where can you place someone
who's severely mentally ill—like Sato, a Japanese-American U.S.
Army veteran. Age twenty, he held tight to his schizophrenic,
bipolar psychotic delusions: That he had HIV. Cancer. An extra X
chromosome. A self-described "small penis and swollen testicles."
Voices in his head. "Something is blocking me!" he would exclaim,
fists pounding his skull. There was just one topic on which Sato had
no delusions—his insanity. "I have never worked due to my condi-
tion," he said. "My family wanted to put me to rest, so they put me
in foster care at age ten." At twenty, he already had a long history of
hospitalizations and antipsychotic injections—not the usual, least
invasive first line of mental health defense.

How do you discharge a kid like this? On the streets, he would
die.

We understood how confused and angry the paraprofessional
staff felt (although I don't think they could say the same about us).
The military had helped them escape poverty, violence, and early
childhood abuse. They had served their country but were lowest in
the chain of command. They felt dishonored and dismissed. The
military is all about uniformity. Now civilian employees, they were
expected to see each veteran as an individual.

Old habits, and lifestyles, die hard. One Dom Assistant had
two open felonies. Another attended VA addiction treatment groups
three mornings weekly, at another VA clinic, while keeping his Dom
job. One stole an iPad from the canteen, the campus sundry store,
and, in a fit of rage, actually bit the female staffer with whom he was
romantically involved.

Penalties for such violations were not stiff, investigations were frequently avoided, and jobs were rarely lost. For example, Richard, an Army vet on staff, himself a graduate of the Domiciliary program, lit a candle in his office one Friday, forgot to snuff it out before leaving for the weekend and caused a fire. His punishment was: a warning issued to the full Dom staff about the importance of following safety protocol. Nothing more.

Why? Most of the Dom Assistants, like Richard, were vets. Some had residual or recurring mental health and substance abuse problems. All worked long, lousy hours and were dead-ended in entry-level DA jobs. In addition, disciplinary action could have perilous consequences; suppose these disgruntled veteran employees filed grievances with their Congressman? And so, as the saying goes, "The VA takes care of its own."

Not so for the pampered elite! Many social workers and psychologists, myself included (more later), were slapped with serious charges by resentful patients and lower-level staff. One psychologist was investigated for sexual harassment after yawning, stretching, and, said a patient, "thrusting out her chest." These formal complaints used up a lot of paper and human resources.

In truth, it is harder to get fired from the VA than to get hired. I don't think the Trump administration, or any administration, will make a dent in the Great Wall of the VA. That's how it is, and how it will always be. When I started working there I was scared, just as I have been at every new job: What if I fail? But a wise soul named Adam, then a VA social worker for twenty years, calmed me down: "You can't get fired!" he said, with a laugh. "You'd have to murder someone. Even then, they'd probably just put you in another clinic."

High Times

Is it asking too much for a substance abuse employee to be sober? At least at work? For months, Larry, a Domiciliary Assistant, made it to work every day despite being in full relapse mode on heroin. I don't know how he did it, and when he did, he didn't offer much. At meetings, he nodded off and snored. In large groups, he sat in the back to avoid fellow workers (who he knew were watching). But sometimes, the meetings were small, with just one veteran and five or six members of the staff. How could my colleagues fail to see, or hear, the (sleeping) elephant in the room? By pretending, of course. By acting. Not I, though. Finished with (childhood) acting—forever!—at the first sound of a snore, I would slam the windows shut to startle him awake. Mind you, these were VA windows, old and heavy, and I labored, like Sisyphus pushing a boulder uphill, to master the task. But it worked. The resulting thud woke up Larry the DA, if only for a short time. I felt sorry for the vets, seated at a conference table, discussing their sobriety alongside an alleged authority figure in a heroin nod.

It was worse with Jared, an addiction therapist and Marine veteran who led substance abuse groups while high on cocaine. For a while, he blamed his excessively runny nose on bad bouts of flu or exposure to anthrax. Eventually he admitted to relapse, took leave (allegedly to get sober), then returned to work at another LA-area VA. Imagine: Vets in substance abuse groups with a therapist who's high. How could they maintain respect? Or hope? Much less sobriety?

Jared looked like a choir boy: Tall. Caucasian. Impeccably groomed. Had he looked more "ghetto," we would have immediately suspected him of abusing drugs. The bias of the elite?

The Homefront

There was sniping on all fronts. Most of it was verbal, although a bullet was once found on an elevator floor, prompting a social worker, a mother of two, to quit.

Swearing and disrespect were forbidden at the Domiciliary,

according to the handbook. But there was plenty of it, loud and clear: "Fuck you! You're a government flunkey!" "Why are you fuckin' looking at me that way?" "You don't get it; you don't know what it's like." "How can you live with yourself?" "I know you think of me as the 'n' word." Et cetera.

It hurt to hear these things, a lot—especially when they were hurled at me, when I was trying so hard to fight both *for* veterans and *against* an impossibly labyrinthine system. Sure, they were just expressing frustration and fear. Of course, I shouldn't have taken their remarks personally. But as the person up front receiving the blows, it hurt.

Here, there was no hiding behind Dr. D's cloak of authoritarianism. Patients had rights. They could wear bedroom slippers all day. They didn't have to walk three miles to AA as they did at the Recovery Treatment Center. They didn't even have to go to AA. They weren't expected to be polite or obedient—nonviolence would suffice.

I was the new kid on the block. I didn't understand this liberal approach. My colleagues tried to explain: The purpose of therapy is to instill motivation and hope, not fear. You have to suck up the patient abuse— some, but not all of it. You have to empathize and consider the pathology underlying the outbursts. These men aren't evil; they're sick. As the Chief put it, when I asked her to reassign a patient I said I couldn't stand: "It's not the person who offends you, It's his behavior." That may sound sappy, but adopting the attitude helped me through some rough times. To this day, I cringe when President Trump labels a school shooter "evil" or "an animal." Even "sicko" is an improvement.

It took me a full four years to toughen up. I first noticed my progress when, walking down the hall, a dark, bearded and obviously furious vet whom I'd never seen before blocked my path and shouted, "You have to give me a letter for the Court!"

Wait a minute. Who are you?

"If you don't give me a letter, I don't need to be here," he shouted again.

Then he got too close for comfort. I stepped back, saying something about first things first, and by the way, what is your name? I asked him to meet with me because "I can't request leniency from the Court for someone I don't know." He sneered beneath the black beard: "If you can't do that, *what do you do*??" I counted to three (or maybe four), smiled, and said: "NOTHING!"

That one word stunned him like a Taser. He left.

This was a milestone. For the first time, I stood my ground and felt unintimidated. By the end of the day, four staffers had called to complain that the guy—whose name I have happily forgotten—was yelling and creating scenes. That night, he went AWOL—Absent Without Leave. He just took off without notice. Several days later, when his parole officer called, I didn't hesitate to say that (1) he left the program; (2) he was extraordinarily difficult; (3) he would not be welcomed back; and (4) he needed a more restrictive environment—like jail. Truly, I wasn't out for revenge, but you can't help everyone, and I most certainly couldn't help him. It's unethical to retain patients you can't effectively treat.

In time, I was able to channel such verbal assaults, and my hurt feelings, into sound clinical thought. For example, when a guy screamed, "You love to control men!" my thought would be something like, "If only I could!" And, "Hey, I'm not your mother or your wife." But what I said was: "What makes you feel that way?" to calm him down. When a vet said, "You can't imagine what I've been through!" my thought would be, "Want to bet? I've heard it a million times." Instead I would respond with, "Tell me more," or "I understand." Those words could puncture the ballooning rage.

Once in a while, though, it was best to surrender. When an elderly, frail man brandishing a cane raised his voice to declare, "I don't let any woman tell me what to do! It's against the Bible!" I prayed for him to leave, suggested he see another (male) counselor and opened the door for his exit.

I understood these veterans' fury, even when I didn't want to hear it. They had served their country. Worn the uniform. Done the drills. Survived boot camp. Engaged in combat. In return, they expected educational benefits. Government monies. Public gratitude, at the very least. Instead, what did they get? Long lines. Long wait times for appointments. A revolving door of interns instead of one reliable MD. A piddling pension. Too much medication. Not enough therapy. "Threshold" or "doorway psychiatry," a term used for the all-too-common practice of doctors prescribing pills for anxiety and depression, in one or two minutes, without fully entering the exam room.

Guilty as charged. That's how it was in the court of veterans' opinion. I was a faceless bureaucrat. A government flunkey. In it for the money (a social worker's salary?!). Uncaring. Bourgeois. There were no softballs or exemptions for a Berkeley liberal and Red Diaper baby, which of course they didn't know about (and wouldn't care, if they did). What they saw in me was: Nice clothes. Nice car. A good job. A woman of means. Guilty as charged.

I tried mindfulness. This is a highly regarded stress-reduction treatment modality for young vets. Rooted in cultures of the Ancient East, it promotes meditation and the principle of "being present" to reduce stress.

Mindfulness benefits clinicians, too. When a guy would scream at me, I would try to turn inward, listen to my breathing and meditate for a moment, then respond rather than react. While resulting in more effective patient care, this tactic also provided a good defense against a common work hazard: "secondary PTSD"—a syndrome, and diagnosis, which all too often hits mental health care professionals, who come to mirror the same symptoms as combat veterans: Anxiety. Anger. Hypervigilance. Et cetera. Listening to tales of trauma every day takes its toll. I still haven't forgotten some:

"My mother took my baby sister's dirty diaper and smeared it over my face."

"There were thirteen of us kids. We were supposed to move. My parents said there wasn't enough room in the car, so they left me behind. They didn't come back. I don't know why."

"In foster care, I was like Mr. Belvedere in that [1970s] TV show about a butler. I was there to serve them. All they wanted from me was the [government] money."

"My mother would get drunk, take her clothes off, then try to bust down my bedroom door and seduce me."

In empathy, I found comfort and calm. I would "feel their pain," as a certain politician used to say, but learned, over a period of years, to dispel at least some of it on the drive home.

Sexual Harassment

We were in process group, fifty guys talking about the interrelationship between drugs and sex: How people rely on stimulants (crack, meth) and depressants (alcohol, benzos) to fuel their drive and calm their nerves. I remarked that some people become sexually dysfunctional without drugs.

Ollie, age seventy, a Vietnam combat vet, didn't seem to understand: "You're saying people can't have sex without drugs and alcohol. You're a married woman. You don't do alcohol or drugs. Are you saying you don't have sex with your husband?"

"What makes you think I don't do alcohol or drugs?"

That was my way of dodging a bullet. I was a woman in a man's world, but these were no ordinary men. They had survived combat in faraway places, prison, drugs, the streets. They had joined the Service to escape home, or to satisfy the Courts, or because they didn't know what else to do. They abhorred political correctness.

They were not aware of sophisticated nuances of language and thought, nor did they want to be. These were homeless vets, smart but with minimal levels of education (a high school diploma, GED or, at most, a two-year AA degree). Some had neglectful parents who themselves suffered from poverty, drug abuse, domestic violence. "My guys"—their adult children—had lived much of their lives on the streets, doing drugs and little else.

That was what they knew.

Against such backdrops, I tried to tread gently. So, for example, I let it go when an angry Mario denied missing the patient community meeting. His proof: "I noticed you there, Mrs. Plate, in a short skirt." I didn't object when the vet suffering from bipolar disorder demanded assignment to another social worker—anyone except Mrs. Plate!—who, he said, "laughs at my low libido." (How did he come up with that?? He was reassigned.) I smiled and walked on whenever the crack addict asked me, "Wanna dance?" and shut him down when he tried to hijack a therapy group on relationships by asking, "Can you call it a relationship when all you want is slam, bam, thank you, ma'am?" I didn't answer the twenty-eight-year-old veteran who had served in Iraq, claiming that "If you haven't had sex on meth, you can't know how I feel." I even waited a long time before complaining about Cleo, the devout Muslim fundamentalist, grief-stricken the day Osama bin Laden was killed. Stressed out, he left the program, then enrolled in another one on VA grounds. From there, he sent sealed, stamped love notes to my Dom mailbox about my "hard, tiny little body" and what he wanted to do with it. Still, I didn't call the program with concern until I read the line: "By your not answering, I am keeping up hope." I called the program chief, and the vet stopped.

What unsettled me more were the sneak attacks. One woman against sixty men. The attacks were verbal, not physical. I found it funny when veterans would proclaim, "I don't hit women!" (despite documented histories of domestic violence) or when they ranted wildly about how you, the VA, Social Security, the world sucked, and worse—but apologized when they used a cuss word: "Excuse my French!"

Otherwise, a female social worker was fair (and easy) game. This became clear to me early on, when I had to tell a room full of veterans at a community meeting that the Domiciliary was instituting mandatory in-house therapy groups—otherwise known as dreaded "Weekend Programming."

Sadly, not all resident vets are truly and deeply committed to therapeutic treatment. They want to be clean, sure, but they may not want to *get* clean by putting in all that hard work. Some prefer to be free after 5:00 p.m. weekdays, most definitely Saturdays and Sundays! They had "stuff to do" that they couldn't get around to Monday through Friday. They resented feeling "policed," 24/7, as they were in the military, or by their wives, or in prison. They voiced fierce objections to mandatory weekend groups: "When do I see my girl if I'm stuck in weekend programming?" or "What about *me* time?" and "Do I ever get a chance to relax?"

One particular morning, at a community staff-patient meeting, a shout came from the back of the packed dayroom: "I'm going to report your ass to patient advocacy!" It was James A, off medications for bipolar disorder, swinging his cane as he made his way through the crowd to where I sat, up front. For a terrifying few seconds I had to wonder: What might he do to me—and to the social work intern at my side? James A had two sons on Death Row. Did he belong there, too? "We'll just see" about my "little announcement" that there would be weekend programming, he said.

This attack launched an avalanche of ill will.

"She's not fit to work with veterans!" shouted a voice from the back.

Then another: "I agree! She doesn't get us!"

In fact, the decision to implement weekend programming came from administrators—not me—but that's what happens when you're in the line of fire.

There was another memorable revolt. They had been lying in wait for me to start a group when...

"We want a male facilitator!"

"We can't say what we want, talk like we want!"

"We can't relate to a woman."

"Only a man can understand us."

"We want to act like ourselves and talk like ourselves."

Their points were valid, but you can't have a meaningful discussion with a mob. That day, I heard them out and tried not to overreact. The next time we met, I brought Greg, a quiet, soft-spoken but no-nonsense veteran on staff. Instantly, the lions became lambs. They were quiet and cooperative. They had no complaints. And when Greg talked, they did not talk back. "Do you want to keep walking the walk, and talking the talk the same way, or are you here to change and listen to someone else?" Greg asked. "You think you know what's good for you? You didn't when you were out on the street!"

Silence.

Intellectually, I understood their behavioral transformations, but they didn't sit well in my gut. "Why do they like to rough me up?" I asked Greg.

"*Because they can*," he said. Simple as that. "This would never happen with a male in the room."

Guilty Until Proven Innocent

At first, I thought it was a joke. "The Gapper"—an administrator who picked on women with stylish clothes and tight blouses gapping between buttons—pulled me by the elbow into the staff bathroom. I expected her to say, in that inimitable schoolmarm style: "They can see your bra!" Or, "You know these guys!" Instead she intoned, "Martin J [a patient] is charging you with sexual harassment!" I laughed and shrugged it off.

Next thing I know, I'm called into the Gapper's office and my boss, the tall, elegant, conservatively dressed African American woman known as "the Chief," steps in, looking very solemn. "I have to pull you from the Domiciliary," she said. "The [VA employee] union called." Together, the two explained: When a veteran submits a formal complaint, especially one alleging sexual harassment, it must be addressed with all seriousness. Staff cannot be favored over vets. The Gapper then read aloud the grievance. According to complainant Martin J, Andrea Plate was discharging him from the program because he rejected her sexual advances. His narrative described me in a white mini-skirt, at every encounter over many months, sitting on the edge of my desk, swinging, crossing and uncrossing my legs ("I don't think she wears underwear," he wrote). He described me as a spurned woman, retaliating by sending him to the streets. In fact, the guy refused to engage in programming or follow any rules, but he did his best to discredit me.

"You can't take this seriously," said the Gapper, giggling as she continued to read aloud.

Sure, I can. Try knocking yourself out at graduate school, accumulating 3200 hours of clinical supervision, then passing a mammoth, two-part state licensing exam, only to be treated like a crack whore/criminal! I left in tears that day. The Chief gave me one day to grieve on paid leave. "It may not seem like it," she said, "but the vets appreciate you." Right. It might not seem like it.

Thus, I was removed from my post and restricted to desk work. I was forbidden to audit my colleagues' therapy groups. I was ordered not to answer knocks on my office door. I was denied all contact with veterans until it could be proven, beyond a reasonable doubt, that I posed no risk to them. But by the law of unintended consequences, a new problem arose: Now instead of three available social workers, there were just two. The boss was worried. If things didn't get done, she, too, would be in trouble. And so, she decided to plead "my" case to the investigatory committee.

Armed with a sketch of my office, she showed the impossibility of the complainant's claim: Even the most physically fit, the most Pilates-prone (as I am), the most flexible human form couldn't possibly conduct an interview and type on a computer while sitting on the edge of a desk, crossing and uncrossing her legs. Three days later, the investigation was called off.

It was a hollow victory. "You know what convinced them you weren't committing sexual harassment?" she said. "Your age." Aha! I was fifty-two. Would a younger woman have been suspect?! Was I too old to feel lust?!

"Once they heard that," she added, "they laughed and said, 'Forget about it.'"

Still, this silly and sordid affair made me paranoid. Sure, I hadn't done anything wrong, but as the saying goes, "Just because I'm paranoid doesn't mean I don't have enemies." Eager to fix "my problem," as I thought of it, I trotted off to Ann Taylor and Banana Republic, where I bought clothes in sizes four or six, rather than the usual two's. Those baggy pants and oversized jackets were a turn-off to men, for sure. But they drew the attention of the few women vets we had, who spotted my cover-up. "You used to wear such cute clothes," they said, making their way up front at the end of a group meeting. "You're wearing these big jackets and you're all covered up." I was wary, at first. Female patients can be aggressive too, but in different ways. They can be caustic and competitive— like Betty, the tall, busty, middle-aged woman with blonde hair piled high on her head, who once gushed, "I wish I had your tiny body! You're so petite!"—only to add, a minute later, "But I'd want *my* boobs!"

Nevertheless, these women, on this day, had the best of intentions.

"We know about that kind of harassment," said Janet, rolling her eyes cynically and nodding her head.

"You can't hide who you are," said Cyndy. "They're guys. *Just guys*. And they're gonna look and say stuff."

I was surprised by several things: the transparency of my literally oversized makeover; how quickly these women caught on to my act; and how, at that moment on that day, their sense of sisterhood transcended the barriers of class and race.

Six months later, I gave my newish size sixes to Goodwill, and started dressing, again, like my "old" self. (Old, as in, who would think of *her* engaging in sexual harassment??)

That was the end of it. Or so I thought. Martin J was discharged a few days later, by a male social worker. Then came Tito Rosa, a former patient suffering from bipolar disorder and PTSD. He had stopped taking his medications, but now, back at the Dom, was ready to "get myself together again." At the end of our assessment meeting, he mused about changes in the Domiciliary, including veterans who seemed "kind of rough around the edges" and disrespectful of staff.

"You know what they told me about you?" he said, with an eye-roll. "That you were accused of sexually harassing a patient. Can you believe that?"

Yes, Tito, I can.

It had been two years.

Vietnam Redux

It wasn't until 2007 that the young ones came home. The first five years, before the trickle-down from Afghanistan and Iraq, most of my patients were in their fifties and sixties—rusty relics of Vietnam who talked a lot about "the Mekong [Delta]," "Cu Chi" (the infamous, 75-foot city of underground tunnels dug by the Viet Cong), and the "mama-sans" who provided comfort in brothels.

Like many of my generation, I was partly mired in the past. So many unresolved emotions! Guilt over the wounded warriors I had once heckled. Pride in my generation for protesting the war. Sadness for the lost idealism of the sixties and early seventies. So when my husband, a journalist and author specializing in Asian-U.S. relations, asked me to select a vacation spot, I answered: Vietnam. Sure, it would be a different country 30-odd years hence. Yes, it had become Westernized. Modernized. Even Americanized. Still, I wanted to go.

It takes a lot for a Red Diaper baby to become a true American patriot. The trip to Vietnam did just that.

On a guided tour of the Cu Chi tunnels, I was the lone Ugly American among hordes of Australians, Singaporeans and Chinese. The tour began with a documentary about "ruthless Americans." Next, a jungle walk showcasing Vietnamese booby traps—"Bye-bye, GI," said the young male tour guide, laughing. "Viet Cong had slim hips! Americans got stuck." Inside the tunnels, a Conga line of tourists, crawling on hands and knees, were treated to a quick taste of combat terror. Yes, it was horrifying—even without rats, without combat gear, without the weight of worrying where, and when, the enemy would strike.

Ho Chi Minh city was fabulous! Glamorous. Lots of neon. A hip, stylish population of more than eight million, many under age thirty-five (so many elders killed off). At the War Remnants Museum, cigarette lighters stolen off of dead GIs were for sale. Photos of grotesquely deformed Vietnamese, courtesy of that deadly U.S. herbicide Agent Orange, were on display. There were none of maimed GIs.

On a daytime cruise down the Mekong Delta, six tourists in a tiny sampan—rowed by a Vietnamese guide, of course—gazed wondrously at the lush green canopy of foliage overhead. "Beautiful," said the husky Australian man up front. But my mind's eye pictured something else: Jesse A, a combat veteran back home, who remembered it as a place where "you could hear a butterfly land on a wet leaf."

Up north, in Hanoi, we toured the Hoa Lo Prison, better known as the Hanoi Hilton, home of the late Senator John McCain for five years during the Vietnam War. Over the years it had morphed into a museum and tourist trap—a dank, dark den of concrete and stone, with massive steel doors and a guillotine (courtesy of the French colonists who built the place to imprison Vietnamese). No, I did not join my husband and step inside a McCain-style cell. Was I paralyzed by fright? Suffering from secondary PTSD? Worried that, by some freakish fluke, the door would slam shut?

This was an emotional line I could not, would not cross.

Welcome Home

I did not disclose to the veterans my vacation destination. I did not want to be accused of "slumming." But word got out, as it always does in small, tight-knit, cloistered communities.

Jet-lagged, my third day back at the VA, community meeting progressed as usual: Sixty veterans and a few staff. Announcements about problems with the heating system. A review of roommate rules. The Thought of the Day patient officer reading aloud the Thought of the Day.

Until the psychologist poked me. Someone had called out my name.

"Come to the front of the room, Mrs. Plate."

It was Claude, ex-Army, a man with a hard face and a soft heart who had served stateside during the Vietnam War.

Standing together before the packed room, he pulled something from behind his back and read aloud: "We now present this

Certificate of Appreciation to Mrs. Andrea Plate, LCSW, Team 1, West LA VA Medical Center, Domiciliary, April 2006. In recognition of your recent visit to Vietnam and in honor of those who served."

Then he put it in my hands. There were those words—those thrilling, utterly shocking, emotionally loaded words—outlined by a squiggly graphic in the shape of Vietnam, drawn on pre-packaged diploma paper, in a black plastic frame still bearing a Rite Aid tag.

Some riches can't be bought.

Shouted one of the guys: "Hey, man, we thought you were away on a beach vacation sipping a piña colada!"

Said another: "You went there?! Even after dealing with us?!"

"It was *because* of you," I explained.

I don't think they understood. And I don't think they would believe that, twelve years later, their certificate of appreciation still hangs on my bedroom wall.

Chapter Three

THE END OF THE BUSH ERA
2007–2008

I adored Chuck, and I don't know why. He wasn't particularly smart, or motivated. Maybe it was the boyish face, the big round eyes and the goofy, toothless grin, but I was not alone in this. Said his social worker at the VA offices in downtown LA, "I love him, too. Doesn't everyone?"

It was 2007. Chuck was fifty-six years old, a Vietnam combat veteran, homeless at least thirty-one years—since his discharge from the Service. For a long time, he enjoyed life on the streets. He knew "all the ritzy people at the hotels." He also knew Nathan, the talented schizophrenic Skid Row cellist and subject of the movie "The Soloist." Steve Lopez immortalized Nathan in a series of columns for the *LA Times*, but Chuck had heard him play years before. He also knew the newsstand vendors who let him read their goods, free of charge. "My favorite is the *New York Post*!" he told me. "The blotter page."

In essence, Chuck was a loner. He left his family decades ago but would not say why. He had hookers, but no friends. He didn't need people, he said, because they were "too much trouble.... On the street, you get burned by them, so it's better not to get close." He might have been a textbook case of "schizotypal disorder," with symptoms like social phobia, social detachment, and paranoid thoughts. Or he could have had PTSD, which in some cases surfaces as "emotional numbing" (an inability to access one's emotions). But

Chuck had no psychiatric diagnosis—because he had no psychiatrist. He wanted no part of medications, or psychiatric treatment, or even substance abuse treatment, despite his long history of abusing alcohol and crack. He wanted housing. Period.

Street life had been good to him—or so he thought, and said. Chuck enjoyed his freedom. He had friends. He was well-known and well-liked. He had a monthly VA pension of $1072, several blankets, one or two changes of clothes, and his very own spot under a freeway bridge. Clearly, Chuck wanted no responsibility of any kind—he'd had more than enough in Vietnam. But now, getting on in years, he said, this lifestyle was starting to take its toll.

Chuck was a lot of work, though. He wouldn't comply with programming, so I customized his care. I didn't make him go to AA meetings, or even to VA substance abuse groups. That angered my colleagues, who believed that "a rule is a rule," but by touting bureaucratic memes like "patient-friendly" and "patient-centered care," I kept them at bay. Instead, I required him to read the Twelve Steps—a step a week, with a handwritten response to each—then read aloud his thoughts and discuss them with me. For twelve weeks, he did just that. He explained that he couldn't believe in a Higher Power he couldn't see (and added that he hadn't seen one since Vietnam). He said he didn't need to make amends because he had "no real friends." It was tortured logic, to be sure, but I marveled at his penchant for self-analysis despite decades of homelessness and drugs. He had a lot going for him: Innate charm; a soft, impish, round face and twinkly eyes; and a sense of humor that was hard to resist.

Since the Service, Chuck hadn't worked. His sole income was his VA pension. For a homeless guy, $1072 a month was enough to get by; but now he was interested in sleeping indoors. To do so, he'd have to save money and stay off drugs. And so, he sobered up on VA grounds, then agreed to discharge to a transitional housing program on LA's notorious Skid Row—a hotbed of downtown homelessness, drug abuse and crime. And yet, none of that worried him. He insisted that he was "fine" with that neighborhood, which he knew so well. Best of all, he would have his own room. So after ninety days in programming, he left.

He missed me, as he said he would, but a month later I lost track of him. Word was, he went back to the streets.

"Move the Bodies"

Until around 2007, there was no therapeutic treatment at the Domiciliary. Veterans were farmed out to other VA clinics on the grounds for mental health care. Thus, the chief function of Domiciliary social workers was to move veterans off government property and into community housing. Such work is called "discharge planning," and it is the lifeblood of social work because, obviously, people cannot stay in transitional housing. Period. It's the social workers who "move the bodies," as the saying goes. But we do other things, too, like assess and refer people to programs, whether for housing, HIV support or legal aid. To do this well, we have to know what the options are for many things, including shelter, clothing supplies, reduced-fee California IDs and cell phones (for eight years called "Obamaphones"); and we have to match them to their needs: A letter to the Court requesting modified payments for child support? Referral to a secular sobriety support group, rather than AA?

Most of all, veterans flocked to us for clothing vouchers and bus tokens (the latter, much treasured in LA, if you don't have a car or your license has been revoked). We also wrote letters of support for Court. All of these fall under the rubric of "case management."

But while clinical care—individual therapy and referrals to psychiatrists who can prescribe medications—is respected, case management is not. Even social work professors fail to understand. "We want our students doing therapy, not case management," said a highly regarded prof from a major Southern California university. Really? She was snooty, all too sure of herself and most definitely out of touch. I wanted to say: Don't your students need jobs?! Don't they have to fit into the mental health care market of today? Name the nonprofit or government institution budgeted for that! In fact, individual therapy is a luxury not just for patients, but for an overwhelmed staff (it most often occurs in private practice).

In actuality, case management requires real clinical skill and talent. You don't send someone to the front lines of Social Security without first learning their personal back story. You wouldn't send someone to live in any neighborhood without knowing his/her drug history as it relates to the proposed environment. And when an enthralled veteran calls you from the courthouse steps to exclaim, "I don't have to go to jail! I can stay in the program!"—you can bet you have established therapeutic rapport.

The mainstay of my job was discharge planning, but I approached it with dread. How do you place veterans in housing who have little to no money? With mental health and substance abuse disorders? With long rap sheets and short rental histories? Under the administration of George W. Bush, the VA was a volume business. Our mandate was to serve as many veterans as possible, quickly—in LA, where we have the highest population of homeless veterans nationwide and an affordable-housing crisis.

The chief options were not ideal:

(1) Transitional or supportive group housing programs in the community, under contract to the VA (otherwise called grant-per-diem programs, or GPD), where the food served garners more complaints than at a college dormitory, as do the bedbugs;

(2) Private or nonprofit sober living homes, a form of housing which is neither VA-approved nor accountable

to government, and, if you believe the vets—I do!—
not always sober environments;

(3) SROs (single room occupancies), most of which are
located in high-rises on or near crime-ridden, drug-
infested Skid Row, thanks to the NIMBY (Not In
My Back Yard) phenomenon; and

(4) "Board and cares," which are low-cost group homes
for the elderly or disabled, and which eat up the full
sum of the veteran's Social Security check as hungrily
as a snake devouring a mouse.

It would be impossible to list all these programs, for a number
of reasons:

(1) There are hundreds of them all over California.

(2) Some are legit (certified nonprofits, government
partnerships), but many are not.

(3) The vast majority are here today, gone tomorrow.
By next week the latest hot spot may become old
news. (The manager may relapse, or leave for a more
lucrative and less difficult job.)

And so, the deck was stacked against both veterans and social
workers. We had too few cards to deal. The game was rigged and
altogether unfair.

What a relief to hear a veteran say, "I'm moving out of state!"
There was no such thing as a VA-sponsored, state-to-state transfer.
Meaning: No further services needed on the California end. The vet
goes on his own. Period. But sometimes, I felt compelled to cross
state lines and argue a case. A cold wind blew in from Hawaii when
I called a social worker at the Honolulu VA: "Don't send him!" she
barked. "This place should be a last resort. Unemployment is high.

Homelessness is high. The state does not, cannot welcome homeless veterans." Then she tried to tame the winds: "You can send him if he has a job, or housing. Don't send him if he has neither."

The veteran in question, a Vietnam combat Marine, was a native of Hawaii who had come to California seeking help.

Blind Justice

One of my most difficult discharges was Jerry, age fifty-five and legally blind. Or so he said. This was not indicated in his medical chart, but he could have been diagnosed by an MD outside of the VA. To consult with that doctor, I would need Jerry's written consent, which he would not provide. Jerry was well-known to the Blind Rehabilitation Services clinic at the VA, which assisted the visually impaired as well as the legally blind. Over time, suspicions surfaced as to what Jerry could—or could not—see. Most worrisome was his roommate's complaint that he couldn't sleep because Jerry "watched" pornography in his room every night on his private TV.

We were all hesitant to confront Jerry. He had a track record of calling his Congressman's office to complain, and when the Congressman's office calls the VA, it is bad news, because: (1) the customer—the veteran—is always right; (2) it would be political suicide to side with the scandal-ridden VA over a homeless veteran; and (3) when they call they often say, "You cannot *deprive a veteran of services*." To me, this meant give him what he wants. Services for blindness? Fine. An evaluation for PTSD? Sure.

But who would be willing to house this guy? He had a meager income from Social Security that he refused to spend on housing. He was comfortable at the Domiciliary, where he was housed and fed, and where he wondered aloud, so all could hear, whether his eyesight was sufficient to keep him safely afloat in a rental, cooking his own meals. After many weeks of negotiations, he finally was accepted, and agreed to go to, a residential program that was very low-cost. Called Bell Shelter, and located in the city of Bell, about an hour's drive southeast of LA, it offered a variety of programs, including one specifically for veterans. That was where Jerry went.

We could not let him travel there alone. For a high-maintenance veteran like Jerry—politically connected and emotionally volatile—we needed what's known as a "warm hand-off""—a safe, smooth bon voyage before he went out on his own. When we got to Bell—yes, I was part of the transfer squad—I followed the advice of the psychologist on the case, who warned me as we took off from the VA, "Don't let him out of your sight when you get there! He might make himself 'accidentally' trip and fall so he has to come back to the VA!" Accordingly, a few hours later, waiting for Bell staff to process the paperwork, I followed this allegedly blind vet's every move, even clutching his elbow while heading down the handicapped ramp for "smokes."

The plan went off without a hitch. Toward the end, the check-in person asked Jerry for written proof of his Social Security income. Instinctively—and no doubt unthinkingly—he got down on his knees to riffle through papers in the large brown cardboard box that held his belongings. "I found it!" he said, holding up a letter-size envelope with the return address, "Social Security," written in very small print. Jerry seemed to have no problem reading it—but I, wearing contact lenses, was forced to squint.

Housing Policy: Under Construction

The road from the VA to LA was anything but smooth. What were politely called "service gaps" seemed like strategic sinkholes. For example:

(1) The system made it difficult to place veterans with "just one" diagnosis. Some transitional housing programs

accepted only those vets with "co-existing disorders," meaning, both mental illness and addiction. *As if one were not enough.* To get them admitted, I had to double their troubles: Yes, he has a drug problem (not since high school, and who didn't, back then?) and a mental health disorder (he occasionally mentions depression). This amateur practice of a little distortion—once accepted by clinicians who could assign them appropriate billing codes—went a long way to help these vets.

(2) No one wanted heroin addicts, however. They were the boogeyman.

Fearful of deaths due to relapse, most programs wouldn't admit veterans currently using heroin (even if they wanted to stop) or who had used within the past few days (but had since stopped). Furthermore, to enter substance abuse treatment a veteran had to commit to methadone maintenance; but the methadone clinic wouldn't admit anyone without "medical clearance." This meant submitting to, and successfully completing, a battery of medical tests. In the interim, the prospective patient had no choice but to stay on the streets.

Jeff and Sandrine were a young married couple, both veterans and heroin addicts in their twenties. She was rail-thin but cute: a pug nose, dark, Hispanic features and a propensity to wear sexy, tight print leggings (usually animal prints) with halter tops. Jeff was less jittery than she, groggy-looking, with sleepy dark eyes, weathered dark skin (in his twenties!) and a five-o'clock shadow all day. The young lovers holed up in motels for weeks, relapsing multiple times, until they were cleared for admission.

In truth, the heroin situation was worse before 2015. Many programs wouldn't accept veterans, even on methadone maintenance, until SAMSHA (the Substance Abuse and Mental Services Health Services Administration, a branch of the U.S. Department of Health and Human Services), threatened to stop funding them.

(3) Service animals are an important therapeutic tool, especially for young combat veterans with "emotional numbing" or excessive paranoia, both symptoms of PTSD. These are "maladaptive coping mechanisms," meaning, they constitute normal, pained responses to abnormal and horrific circumstances, like losing buddies in combat. Service pets in fact provide emotional healing across species. Only dogs, however, are certified service animals under the Americans with Disabilities Act.

And yet, not all dogs, at all times, were welcome. One veteran and his dog were accepted to a transitional housing program, but their admission was put on hold because the program had a dog quota of two. (I am not making this up.) Since two dogs were already housed there, my veteran—and his dog—had to wait for a vacancy. It was a cold, cruel day, literally, when I was forced to tell a returnee from Afghanistan, age thirty-four, calling me from a street corner during a downpour, that the program manager "hoped" to have an available slot in a few days. "I need a place now!" he said. "Where I go, she [the dog] goes!" He cried and hung up. That was the last I heard from him.

Another sad case involved an elderly man who showed up shortly after his male lover died. He had been

sleeping in his car with a cat named Tiger. No program
would admit the cat, so the old man returned to his car
and his cat. (I think I might have shed a few tears over
this case on the way home that night.)

Yes, service animals presented problems: Fleas.
Diseases. Aggression. But you couldn't always blame the
dog. In one case, a young combat vet in a community
program was caught in an act of bestiality with the house
therapy dog. As punishment, he was forced to vacate his
single room, move in with someone else and leave the dog
alone. Simple. Then the dog got a measure of distance
and some canine therapy. My argument was, if you
supply veterans with dogs, supply the dogs with proper
homes, too!

(4) Veterans who served during a "theatre of operations"
or wartime (Vietnam, Desert Storm, Operation Iraqi
Freedom, Operation Enduring Freedom) are eligible for
NSC (non-service connected) pension. This means that,
if indigent and unemployable, they qualify for monthly
checks in the amount of $1072. But rules are made to
make things difficult, it seems. Veterans who stay at the
Domiciliary, a federal government program, will lose
their pension unless they leave within three months. By
government logic, it is unethical to receive subsidies from
two federal sources— pension benefits *plus* room and
board. Why the cut-off at three months (instead of two,
or four)? No one seems to know, although it is said they
have been working to change the policy since the 1930s.

Where there is a loophole, a resourceful social worker
will find it. This was the heart of my job. Some of those
vets left the Domiciliary just one day, or at most a week,

then returned for another three months. (How's that
for streamlining government!). Worse, veterans who
receive Supplemental Security Income (SSI), which is
Social Security for the indigent (not for a physical or
mental disability), can't even enter the Dom without fully
forfeiting that income. Again, this is considered "double
dipping" from two federal sources (the VA and Social
Security).

No wonder the "D" word (discharge) induced panic
and rage. Scared, veterans would lash out with words—
"That's bullshit! You want to make me homeless again?"
and become mildly violent, slamming the door so my
wall calendar fell, or my nerves did a dance. The next step
was to lock that door, and wait, without moving, for the
sound of their stomping footsteps to fade away.

Nice Guys Finish First

At first, I felt truly sorry for Ron L. He was small, very slight and
fragile-looking, with black marble-like eyes that shone against his
pale skin. Weeks earlier, his male lover had died, which meant he
lost the home he had lived in rent-free for five years. Ron had no
family ties or close friends, having preferred, instead, the exclusivity
of domestic bliss. In addition, he was HIV-positive. What he wanted
and needed most, when he came to me, was a place to live. This was
a tough case, but not atypical. His sole income was less than $900
(from SSI), so he faced a cruel choice: retain his income and leave
the premises, or stay but forfeit the money.

Lucky me. I was the first person to break the news to this poor
veteran. Understandably, he screamed, "You can't do that! Fuckin'
government!" His face grew flushed and he trembled. I knew at that
instant what I had become to him: The Face of "Government." A
flunkey. A messenger of bad news.

Furious, he pivoted on his heels and headed to the door, opened it slightly, then stopped, turned around, slammed the door shut behind him and headed toward my desk. He leaned across it, just a few inches from my face, and spit out the words: "You're a lying cunt! If I ever see you again…" He whipped around and left.

The shock and hurt came later. First, I called VA police. Situated about a half-mile from the Domiciliary, they were the only security force available in situations like this. There were no guards at the Domiciliary. A man so distraught might endanger himself, or others. The police agreed to do a lookout, and evidently followed through, because later that day they escorted him off VA grounds. But I stayed nervous for days. Words like that are hard to forget. The next morning, still spooked, I read his chart to determine his whereabouts. The frail, thin, bereaved HIV-positive vet walked into a West Hollywood police station that night and begged them to let him sleep in a cell. His wish was granted, for one night.

This was a lousy outcome for us both. Nobody won. But by then I was done with him, having learned something invaluable from the experience: never accept degradation or abuse from patients. That is empathy to excess.

Make no mistake. I'm plenty vulnerable. If that vulgar, sexist word had been thrown in my face by a different veteran—not this featherweight guy, but a mountain of macho flesh with a history of felony assault, let's say, or a star sniper from Iraq, or someone just released from the penitentiary—I would have been much more shaken.

Similarly, I found a note under my door one day that read: "Be careful. Someone is talking about putting a chemical compound in the gas tank of your car." I laughed it off, but the few people I showed it to insisted that I make a report to the VA police—so I followed orders, detailing the veteran's purported plan to blow me up, as well as his motivation (he was being discharged). They visited the angry veteran in his room, where he admitted making that state-ment—more than once. Then the cops warned him that such words constitute "a terrorist threat on federal government property." He disappeared the next day, but a few years later came back for treat-ment—fortunately, on another floor, with another social worker.

To this day, I wish I had known the identity of the veteran who wrote the tip-off note. Thanks to him, I was alive and in one piece.

Chapter Four

A NEW COMMANDER-IN-CHIEF
2008–2012

The Independence Movement

Between 2009 and 2011, the federal government began to discourage us from sending veterans to transitional housing programs. It was the dawn of a new era. Our new president, Barack Obama, set a new goal: to eliminate veteran homelessness by the end of his first term, in 2012. Why the sudden change? Vets in transitional housing programs counted as "homeless," since they were not paying rent. As such, those placements were "bad [housing] outcomes." Government focus shifted to independent, affordable housing.

This new policy, called "Housing First," was the direct opposite of the Bush doctrine, which held that treatment should precede housing. Like my peers, I too missed the hard Bush line (on this one policy point). But according to the National Alliance to End Homelessness, Housing First "prioritizes providing permanent housing to people experiencing homelessness, thus ending their homelessness and serving as a platform from which they can pursue personal goals and improve their quality of life. This approach is guided by the belief that people need basic necessities like food and a place to live before attending to anything less critical, such as getting a job, budgeting properly, or attending to substance use issues." Fair enough.

Such public-policy thinking parallels famed psychologist Abraham Maslow's hierarchy of needs, based on the premise that essential, foremost physiological needs (housing) must be met first, rather than more refined needs (creativity, sobriety) in the pursuit of happiness.

I had grave doubts. Wouldn't that proverbial "roof over the head," unsupported by a foundation of sobriety and mental health, crumble? No matter. I had my marching orders: Find housing vouchers for veterans and send them off… even if you think it's a bad idea.

The linchpin to this new approach was HUD-VASH, or VA Supportive Housing. This was the VA's version of "Section 8," by which the government (Housing and Urban Development) offers rental assistance to landlords as an incentive to provide low-income/affordable housing. With this program, a veteran could get his own apartment in LA, whether in a building earmarked as Section 8 housing or an individual unit in a standard apartment setting.

For veterans sprung from prison or rehab, or just off the streets, the VA's version of Section 8 became the Holy Grail. They felt emboldened and entitled: "I want my own apartment! I'm programmed out! I don't want treatment!" "I don't want to live with other people!" One vet even threatened to commit suicide if he didn't qualify, saying he would leave behind a one-word note: "VASH," the famed acronym. (He did not follow through.)

Even Joe E, a fifty-year-old Hispanic male, a longtime alcoholic who had enjoyed decades of homelessness, sought this kind of housing. For years, life on the streets in downtown LA, near Pershing Square, had been "fine," he said, because "I had no responsibility and I liked drinking." Anxiety? "There was none. I could just drink and relax." But homelessness gets harder with age, he explained, and now that his liver hurt, he was "scared."

There was almost nothing he wouldn't do for a low-cost apartment paid for, in large part, by the government. Joe didn't want treatment, but he vowed to go through it to enhance his housing application. He even got married in order to obtain an affordable apartment. How? In group one day, he explained: He had married his sister's lesbian lover after the two women broke up. The sister moved out, Joe moved in. By marrying Joe, the lesbian-turned-new-lywed got revenge against her former lover (Joe's sister), while Joe got to move into his new wife's apartment, which she had been living in, courtesy of the joint VA/HUD program. After the inevitable divorce, Joe had to apply for a new place.

The pressure to meet housing statistics was so great, and so highly charged both emotionally and politically, that standards of patient care took a dramatic hit. They had to. That old, familiar social work bargaining chip—stay sober or lose your housing—was gone. If the vet in an apartment didn't disrupt the building with loud partying all night, he could stay. If he got loaded, he could stay. He could not be forced into treatment, but he could be enticed to vacate for three months in the event of severe relapse. Then he could return to his place in ninety days (yes, he'd have to pay rent those three months). In this way, "the numbers are good," it was often said, for those classified as "permanently housed." Perhaps the most remarkable report I read during that time, written by a poor, beleaguered social worker, stated: "The veteran must agree to be sober while being *transported* to his unit."

About-Face!

Politicians took years to debate and establish policy. On a day-to-day basis, we hardly knew what was going on. Then suddenly, one day, our marching orders were reversed. That's what happened one Friday afternoon with Adam L, a sad, fifty-seven-year-old Vietnam Era, noncombat veteran whose toothless mouth folded deeply into his sunken face. With sparse white hair and a rail-thin frame, he looked more like a centenarian or a plucked chicken than a wounded warrior. Adam suffered from severe "degenerative disc disease" (back pain), for which he took prescribed narcotics. These eased the physical pain, but he became addicted to them and severely depressed. Adam frequently bemoaned his fate. "Nobody wants me," he sobbed, citing four ex-wives as evidence.

Nevertheless, that Friday morning I told him to prepare to leave the Domiciliary for transitional housing, within a week. He had already stayed eight months—double the approved length of stay—and, as we were so often told (during Bush times), no veteran was permitted to indefinitely "fill a bed while waiting for housing." But at 4:15 p.m. on Friday, while closing out my email, I noticed a new message from the Domiciliary Chief: "Effective immediately, veterans with vouchers for VA Supportive Housing can extend their stay [at the Domiciliary] until permanently housed." Just like that!

Over the weekend, I had to determine the least embarrassing way to explain the about-face. After all that VA-speak about rules, and the therapeutic need to move on in life (and out of the Domiciliary), come Monday morning, I'd be telling Adam L: "No problem. Stay until your apartment is ready." Talk about being undermined! Plus, word would get around: the social workers around here don't call the shots. Don't worry about what they say. Every veteran would assume he could stay, indefinitely, at government expense.

No Easy Fix

Like ants swarming over chocolate cake, newly employed social workers flooded into Housing and Urban Development/VA Supported Housing. That annoying acronym, VASH, sounded both violent and final, when it should have sounded hopeful and beckoning. The new social workers flooding into our system were everything we could hope for: young, just out of social work school, and eager for that first job. But what a job!

In addition, some social workers were detailed to VASH from other VA departments, so the message was clear: The big push now is to improve housing statistics, and don't you forget it. At one time, I heard, VASH social workers had one hundred veterans on their caseloads—but no individual offices or phones. Staff turnover was rampant. Even some of the VA's finest, like my friend Sam—middle-aged, with terrific therapeutic skills and training in all the favored treatment modalities—quit, without the promise of another job. Some took social work jobs elsewhere. A few went into real estate.

In 2011, I couldn't stand to watch the State of the Union address. I couldn't stand the sight of President Obama or Congress. Neither could some of my colleagues, even the African Americans, so excited by his election in 2008 that they had decorated their desks and walls with photos of the First Couple. They had voted for Obama. I had, too. But this administration was asking us to do the impossible: Find permanent housing for thousands of veterans who had been homeless for decades, within a few months, while also making sure they were secure and safe. Without enough funding. Or staffing. (Yes, Congress grew the VA budget, but it was never enough, especially with the young troops coming home).

The VASH Program was a broken system for broken people concocted by policy wonks in Washington divorced from reality. And everyone—patients as well as staff—knew it.

Hate at First Sight

Gary W needed help but accepted none. He hated me from the start. I'm not sure why. Sometimes, it's just the way you look, or who the patient imagines you to be. He refused to speak to me and darted angry stares my way when I said hello.

I knew a few things about Gary. One, his diagnosis was "schizotypal disorder." This is a personality disorder marked by social isolation and emotional detachment. Two, he was stocky and short, with a big head. I never noticed, but according to his psychiatrist, Gary's oversized head caused him to shrink within himself. Traumatized and mocked as a kid, he had developed "social phobia," which, as its name suggests, connotes discomfort with personal relations. Three, the veteran had a long history of severe depression. For days, he stayed in bed. He had no social ties or community connections. Four, Gary was focused on just one thing: Getting his own apartment, and staying there—on a monthly income of $221 from General Relief. It was a terrible plan! Even other vets pleaded with me to help "that guy next door... Please, Mrs. Plate, don't let him go out there!" (As if I had the power to stop him.)

But the VASH social worker had a different agenda. Her job, as she described it to me, was to "put him in housing." Gary got his apartment, moved in, and about five months later returned to the Domiciliary for treatment. He still had his apartment, because his supportive housing counselor negotiated for it to remain vacant while he underwent VA treatment. He continued to pay rent, and, upon program completion, returned home... as if nothing had changed. (And quite possibly, nothing did.)

The System is Broke

Some would say Gary was lucky. At least he had his own place. Many others did not, for all sorts of reasons: Congress, not the VA, defines "chronic homelessness," and in peculiarly precise terms! A veteran who accepts the hospitality of family or friends—*even just one night on a couch*—loses his status as "chronically homeless" and is disqualified from low-cost affordable housing. (Congressional logic: If someone puts you up for one night, they can do so again; you have sufficient social support to avoid the streets). To qualify for such housing, a veteran must supply documentation proving he has had several "episodes" of homelessness within the past three years, or one so-called unbroken episode within the past year. It is a sad truth that some veterans live on the street in order to become eligible. Most amazing of all: People who have access to running water are not considered homeless! Even in prison or jail! Look at it this way—rather, Congress' way—prisons and jails have running water. Therefore, veterans behind bars are not homeless!?

Southern California's affordable-housing crisis is one of the worst in the nation. Nationally, the number of affordable apartments for low-income families fell by 60% between 2010 and 2016. One exception: LA, which has the largest homeless veterans population in the country. In early 2018, the *Los Angeles Times* published an editorial calling this "a national disgrace." Really? They just noticed??

What's more, the homeless crisis is worse than the housing crisis. This was obvious every day. Scores of vets failed at living independently because they had little to no experience managing money, staying sober or developing, much less maintaining, safe and healthy social support. Under the Bush administration, a vet needed $2000 in savings and a steady source of income to qualify for affordable housing. Most couldn't meet that standard so they didn't fail, simply because they never got the chance to try.

Under the Obama administration, all that changed. A man on General Relief could qualify for a HUD/VA Supported Housing apartment, but how could he also pay utility and grocery bills? Not to mention that being in receipt of GR—a whopping $221 per month—is demoralizing and counter-therapeutic. Unsurprisingly, many who landed apartments ended up like Gary, back in treatment, because they had lost, or were at risk of losing, their apartments.

It was both funny and sad. Admissions interviews at the West Los Angeles VA, and probably at the hundred plus VA Medical Centers nationwide, were like class reunions, abundant with warm hugs, friendly greetings and lots of high-fives. Alternatively, some guys showed up embarrassed and ashamed: "Sorry to disappoint you, Mrs. Plate. I wasn't ready… I fucked up."

These negative outcomes were entirely predictable. Sustained recovery is a rare thing indeed, even with treatment completion, and especially on the first try.

It might be easier—and most certainly faster—to sneak past Border Patrol than to land a veteran in an affordable apartment. Inevitably, landlords posed a hard line of questioning: What's the proposed renter's criminal history? Why has he been homeless all these years? Is there a history of eviction? Is he using drugs or alcohol?

To make matters worse, there was no steady stream of housing vouchers. One month we would be flooded with tens of thousands, but then the stream would dry up and there were none. Like shoppers in a grocery store check-out line, everything proceeded apace—until suddenly the lane closed and business stopped. Overnight. Until further notice. With no explanation.

Who was to blame? Housing and Urban Development? The VA? Or both? Those of us on the frontlines didn't know; and these agencies didn't tell. But it was pretty clear: Funding had run out. Someone, at some level of government, hadn't been keeping track, even as the demand for low-cost housing far exceeded the supply.

The End of the Honeymoon

Strange! When I arrived at work one day at 8:00 a.m., scores of veterans were emerging from tents pitched on VA lawns. Then I remembered: This was the second day of a "stand-down" orchestrated by the offices of Los Angeles Mayor Eric Garcetti.

In June of 2014, two years after the President missed his 2012 deadline to eliminate homelessness among veterans, then First Lady Michelle Obama launched a nationwide "Mayors Challenge to End Veteran Homelessness." Los Angeles took on the challenge by organizing a series of stand-downs —makeshift open-air markets on VA parking lots, designed to lure veterans into services and programs. For this particular stand-down, vets had been bussed in from Skid Row the night before and encouraged to stay overnight in tents on VA grounds. Staff members manned booths, promoted their homeless/treatment programs and distributed free goods (cell phones, backpacks, socks). Domiciliary staff stood guard to conduct impromptu screenings and same-day admissions, although few veterans chose to enter treatment. Instead, they scooped up the free merchandise, then took the bus back to Skid Row. What the politicians didn't understand is this: patients don't come ready-made. They need skilled therapeutic interventions to enhance their motivation for long-term sobriety, mental health treatment and, ultimately, the adult responsibilities of working and paying rent. Bad as the street is, it's something they at least know, and where they know others.

In essence, the stand-downs were much ado about nothing. In its 2017 survey, HUD announced a 1.5% increase in veteran homelessness the previous year—the first rise since 2010. In 2018, the LA Homeless Services Authority homeless count was inching toward 53,000 in Los Angeles County (the first actual decrease in four years—but nevertheless far too many to accommodate with housing).

Seeing is Believing

We had to "move the bodies," they said, and if we couldn't land a veteran in his own apartment, well, then, we had to send him somewhere else… even, alas, transitional housing.

Most social workers never see these places. Who has the time? And who truly wants to see? I suppose it's easier to command people into battle than to see the battlefield firsthand. I hated it when brash statements rolled off of administrators' tongues, like, "Send him to a shelter! If he doesn't want to go, that's on him! We're [the VA] in the clear!" Even a psychologist who should have known better, eager to achieve "good discharge numbers" as a route to promotion, took to saying, "Sober livings are perfectly fine!" Really? How did she know? I handed many men slips of paper bearing street addresses and program titles, never to see them again. They vanished, as if down a rabbit hole.

Where did they go? I decided to see for myself.

On the Skids

A native of LA, I had never seen Skid Row, downtown LA's ghetto for the so-called underclass—until 2001, when the UCLA School of Social Work sent the class of 2002 on a walking tour. That's an embarrassing admission, but many Los Angelenos haven't seen Watts Towers either and, for that matter, how many New Yorkers visit the Statue of Liberty?

Our walking tour was led by an iconic figure, herself a resident of the Row—a warm, outgoing, African American woman we followed on early morning rounds as she gave residents hugs and clean needles, met casually with some men outside of a soup kitchen cuddling a four-week-old puppy, and cheered the guy across the street who shouted to her, "I got one month clean today!" We even stopped to speak to a man lying face-up on the sidewalk, after our guide introduced us. "Are social workers like parole agents?" he asked, then laughed when we answered with a resounding "no." Overall it was a small community of like-minded homeless souls looking out for one another because no one else would. They knew each other's names. They said "hi" on street corners.

Granted, this was just one lovely morning under unarmed guard. Yes, Skid Row is a sad, seedy place—to live in. Locals can expect to be robbed or stabbed. Ground-floor bathrooms of grand, historic LA hotels are locked to keep out the homeless. Drug addicts and alcoholics loll around on sidewalks, asleep or semi-conscious. But Skid Row is a true community, more than my neighborhood in West LA, where the only thing that joins us is a zip code. I was sad that night. I wanted to go back—with a community guide, of course, under the auspices of UCLA, and with nonprofit staffers protecting us at each stop.

Years later, I went back on my own (no guard this time), against the counsel of my VA colleagues. They warned that it was dangerous, that I shouldn't go alone, that I was nuts to put myself front and center of all that crime!

In truth, there were some unanticipated challenges. When I first turned onto San Julian Street, which is the main drag of Skid Row, I had to jam on the brakes. People were milling in the street, unfazed by my car (a Mercedes Benz, I confess). A few stood, immobile, like figures in a wax museum—obviously strung out on heroin.

Others were simply oblivious. This was *their* street, no one else's, and if you weren't the police you didn't count. I waited a few tense minutes for a sliver of space to open up, then made a sharp left into some kind of parking lot. There was no ticketing machine, no kiosk and no attendant asking for pay. Whatever. I had come to see some things, so I left the car, hoping for the best, and strolled down Skid Row.

That part was easy. I was not mugged. I was not offered drugs. Probably the navy-blue blazer (military-style) and pearl earrings were off-putting. On Skid Row, you are perceived to be a local, a narcotics agent or some kind of lunatic best to avoid. The latter would be me.

I headed to "Weingart," formally known as the Weingart Center for the Homeless. This was a faded fortress on the corner of Skid Row's Sixth and San Pedro, eleven stories high, with a parking lot surrounded by a chain-link fence. The Weingart Foundation is a big name on the homeless scene. Founded in 1983 by a wealthy real estate couple, it quickly became a huge hub of activity and services offering housing, substance abuse treatment, vocational rehabilitation and case management for all of LA's homeless (reportedly 20,000 per year). The Weingart program also offers transitional housing reserved for vets. Nevertheless, I had a very hard time getting veterans' consent to move into this place on Skid Row, or anywhere near it. This was especially true for those recently sprung from drug treatment or jail. They didn't want "all that," they said. Mostly, they wanted freedom from accountability, no questions asked. And they hated the sordid surrounding street life; who wouldn't? Those who ultimately relented went to Weingart for the promise of (1) their own room, and (2) the right to smoke cigarettes in it.

I also visited a few SROs (single room occupancies)—cheap hotels like the Cecil and the Russ, with long, dark halls; rooms about as big as library carrels; and staff so suspiciously concerned about my safety that when I left they escorted me down the elevator, to the street, and then to the parking lot (the car was still there!), where they stood watch, like my mother used to, until I drove off.

Some weeks I visited places far from Skid Row, but nowhere near the tony neighborhood of Brentwood surrounding the VA. At the Hollywood branch of the faith-based nonprofit Volunteers of America (VOA), for example, I saw a newer program serving a newer model of vet—returnees from Afghanistan and Iraq. This VOA was located in a small stucco building in hip West Hollywood, on the corner of Sunset and Western, next to a Korean church, about a half-hour drive from the VA. I brought along Anna, then a newly hired, twenty-four-year-old VA social worker who had interned there. I did so to be nice—we always need more social workers!—but her presence paid off, big-time.

An army of young, hyper-masculine men answered the door, strutting their stuff in shorts and wife-beater shirts, a mass of bulging muscles covered in tattoos. They hugged her, then seated us in their circle of chairs as they awaited the start of "group." (By myself, I'm sure, I would have been seen as a high school chaperone.) Things were pretty serene—polite chit chat, Bella the house therapy dog making the rounds for strokes—until a door slammed hard and we heard a male voice shout from the outdoor patio. The words were indecipherable but the cry was loud, and sounded violent.

At the same time, the VOA program manager emerged to shake hands. He was a Marriage and Family Therapist (MFT) employed by the community partner program, not the VA. As if nothing had happened—although I'm sure he heard the shout—the MFT led us to his office for a program briefing that was interrupted minutes later, when two residents showed up at the door with a carving knife. They explained that the angry veteran had thrown it. Despite all of my experience—or perhaps because of it—I was spooked. Where was the knife, I asked? In the kitchen, they said.

This surprised me. At the VA, that knife would have been confiscated right away. Said the program manager, "We are not going to deprive veterans of their right to have knives in their kitchen because of one guy! That wouldn't be a fair policy." Policy? Who's talking policy? I'm talking about a carving knife in a kitchen drawer, unlocked and easily accessible to that guy, or any other guy, suffering from an adjustment disorder, PTSD, traumatic brain injury, or who knows what?!

Obviously, this was not my program and not my case, but I urged the MFT (the VA refuses to "recognize," i.e., hire, MFTs) to halt our briefing and address the matter. In a stab of conscience, I guess, he agreed, so Anna and I left. In truth, I didn't want to endure a violent scene, even as a witness, or to distract the MFT from handling this risky situation quickly and safely. And let me be frank: I didn't want to be blamed, in any way. We got enough of that at the VA, whenever anything went wrong.

I didn't learn much about VOA Hollywood that day, but I learned something else, and it shocked me: I was proud to be part of the Veterans Administration. Every day, we faced high-risk situations like that, and knew just how to manage them. As first responders, we were probably unbeatable. At long last, I could see the positive side to all that government-bred paranoia and account-ability. We had a heightened awareness of risk. We were fast and hypervigilant. In the long run, we might have even helped save a few lives.

The Haunted House

If a sober living is "not sober," what is it?

The House of Hope was a sober living home that accepted heroin addicts on methadone. Few did, so it was a must-see. "Dixie, the program manager," as she described herself over the phone, agreed to take me on a tour. There were actually three LA-area Houses of Hope, so she requested that I first stop at "headquarters." This proved to be a tiny, ramshackle office on the corner of Wilshire and North Normandy, near Koreatown and close to a Metro Rail stop—not Skid Row, but no place a woman could stand alone on a street corner without being catcalled.

Dixie failed to show up that morning. Instead, I was met by a bizarrely thin, wiry, fast-talking man with eyes like light bulbs short-circuiting at each thought—no doubt strung out on crack or meth. The "office" was a small, airless space, as smoke-filled as the air outside an AA meeting, so after fifteen minutes, when Dixie was still missing in action, I said I would go myself to visit the House of Hope.

"No, you can't do that!" he said, eyes popping. "You'd need a key." But he refused to hand his over, because he could not leave "the office." Well, since the street was open to the public, I reminded him, I could at least view it from outside. Then I left.

The House of Hope was a nondescript-looking house, two stories, with a Mustang parked on the weedy lawn out front, despite
ample space on the street. To my great surprise, no sooner did I step
out of my car than the front door of the house opened and a man
emerged—the man I had just left behind! He who had just told me
he couldn't leave the office unattended. How did he get there so
fast—by a back route? If so, why?

"I didn't want you going in alone," he said. "These are some
tough guys and they may not be dressed." I could do without the
naked part, but tough guys? Didn't he know I spent my days with
guys like that, wet-haired and half-dressed, cursing and crying in
the halls, as if I didn't exist? Or not caring if a woman stood there,
watching?

The House of Hope was no Club Fed (as the vets called the
Dom). The trek upstairs to the residents' bedroom was harrowing.
With my guide in tow (let's call him Mr. Eyes, since he refused to
divulge his name), I made my way up the spiral staircase, three-
inch heels sinking into crumbling wood with each step, the banister
wiggling under my grip. It was a sunny morning, so when Mr. Eyes
first opened the bedroom door I was blinded by the dark. "VA here!
Woman here!" he shouted. Squinting, I could discern, barely, a
small room packed with bodies in bunk beds, maybe six or seven
guys. But no one seemed to hear the alert, or to stir—except one
man who lifted his head from the pillow, tilted backward, the whites
of his eyes shining in the dark for a second until they closed again,
and his head fell back.

That was the tour. Mr. Eyes helped me down the stairs and
extended a jittery hand to shake goodbye. Driving back to work,
the residual smell of stale cigarettes mixed with sweat clung to my
clothes and my hair. *What exactly was that place?*

"A controlled crack house," a recovering paraprofessional at
work explained. "You can use and live there, and it's better than the

street." Later that day, I told a supervisor: "We cannot send anyone there. Ever!"

His response, without asking why: "Tell the other social workers."

The last I heard, vets called it "The House of Dope."

No Fun

I went to another sober living house on West Washington Ave., which seemed like a lovely suburban area, although veterans told me later that the streets just around the corner were "awful." Maybe I was charmed by the rocking horse on the lawn in front of the yellow house next door to the sober living, or the fact that it was so close to an MTA stop—very convenient for vets with DUIs, without cars and without driver's licenses. A quaint, five-bedroom, two-story home enclosed by a gated, chain-link fence, inside it was impeccably clean and, by the manager's description, tightly run—to the extent that it scared veterans away. "It's like the military," guys would say, who wanted no such reminder of the past. Mandatory in-house meetings, including a Sunday morning AA, household chores, and house meetings—this was all too much for men frightened of facing adult life, for the first time, after years of homelessness and lawlessness.

Another thing the veterans didn't like: the aura that only the best and the brightest deserved to live there. Admission criteria were steep: a steady income (disability pay, pension), because the rent was $800 per month; or a job; or sincere work readiness with the pressure to find a job, quickly. Too much, too soon.

Last Call

Marshall R couldn't go to any of these places. He was too sick and too frail. He was a small guy, maybe five feet four, haggard, with a sharp nose poking out from the loose, sallow skin of his emaciated

face. Marshall was fifty-nine, and had only recently stopped drinking. He was on dialysis due to severe, terminal liver cirrhosis. He
also suffered from "hepatic encephalopathy," a brain disorder asso-
ciated with liver decay, resulting in cognitive dysfunctions such as
agitation, delirium, confusion, stupor and psychosis.

Marshall needed "a higher level of care." That's VA-speak for a
sad, unspoken reality—he's either dying, or at the very least unable
to live on his own. Such patients are referred to "board and care"
facilities, which are low-cost, group housing placements for the
elderly and disabled. To Marshall, any board and care was tanta-
mount to Death Row. He said he would rather live on the street, or
in a car (if only he had one). But after much talk and deliberation,
we reached an agreement to visit a board and care home in Gardena,
a city located in southwest LA.

I drove him in a government car, barely able to see above the
steering wheel. Per standard safety protocol, Marshall took the
backseat. I had been forewarned: An erratic veteran prone to panic
or rage, in the passenger seat, might grab the steering wheel—or the
driver. The end goal was not just to find housing for the veteran, but
for the social worker to return to the VA alive.

I can't remember the name of the place—something like
Gardena Gardens, or Garden Manor. It was cold and antiseptic, as
was the welcoming crew. This is how it works: You show up with a
severely disabled guy who knows he is going to die; who is clinging,
understandably, to what little is left of his income and his life; who
has no family willing to claim him; and no power to alter his fate.
The health technician and receptionist who greet us ask solely about
the sum total of his monthly check: Does he get it regularly? Does
he understand that the facility will take it in full?

(I wouldn't want to go there; would you?)

On the plus side, Gardena Gardens, or Manor, seemed pretty
safe, and there was a "dialysis place" down the street, so by the

time we left, Marshall seemed resigned to go there—almost. He was markedly quiet on the drive back, but on climbing out of the car said, "Thank you for going above and beyond."

At 8:00 a.m. the next morning, there was a knock on my office door. It was Marshall. "I won't go!" he said. That was the gist of his rant. Wild-eyed, lips curled into a semi-snarl, I saw the "other Marshall," the one his fellow veterans had kept hidden, fearing we'd put him in the hospital under four-point restraints. For months, they said, his behavior had been erratic. They frequently found him wandering the grounds at night, disoriented. Once, they pulled him off of a VA bench, waiting for the bus, in his underwear. There's a lot of ruin in a person.

Fortunately, a psychologist rounded up Marshall and his peers for an emergency intervention. They urged him, albeit tenderly, to stick with the plan. Marshall left the next morning, smiling and waving goodbye. A "peer technician" (a veteran now on staff) drove the departing patient in order to execute "a warm hand-off"—once again, as with the questionably "blind" Jerry, this is VA vernacular, and practice, meaning, keep your eyes on the patient until you relinquish custody, shake hands with both patient and staff, then leave—without a trace of liability.

It was a short-term living arrangement. About ten months later, Marshall died of liver disease.

Over the Top

In my sixth year, I got into trouble again. Looking back, I guess I had a few things to prove: That I wasn't a government flunkey; that my spirit could not be crushed; that I would not, and could not, become the establishment sell-out I had protested against in my idealistic college years.

Long before my time, there had been a massive theft of medical records from the "Chart Room." It was obviously an inside job that served no purpose other than to entertain rule-breakers by freaking out the powers that be. As punishment, all staff keys to the Chart Room were confiscated. Only the two clerks who ran the room kept their keys: Dean, a smiley-faced, very overweight Caucasian guy who bided his time viewing oddball online sites—he once treated me to a display of obese squirrels—and Rhonda, a sullen, surly, poker-faced African American woman who quite obviously didn't want to be there, and let you know it by an assortment of eye-rolls, grimaces and grunts. Together, they were Palace Guards who kept watch over the charts—and the staff—who needed to get into that room every day. (For years, before full computerization, we were required to print out and store computer notes in the Chart Room's thick, three-ring binders, one for every Domiciliary resident.)

The two Palace Guards seemed to enjoy their power. So why did they seem unhappy, even resentful? Sometimes they opened the door for us quickly. Sometimes they took a suspiciously long period of time to do so and, on one memorable occasion, they didn't open it at all. That time the two chose instead to watch our distressed faces through the long, horizontal window above the ledge outside the Chart Room. Always pressed for time, we social workers were at their mercy. With the overload of federally mandated paperwork— biopsychosocial assessments, medication lists, interdisciplinary treatment plans—who had time to wait, for anything? But as the VA saying goes, "If it isn't documented, it didn't happen." And at that time, there had to be documentation in both the computer and the kingdom of the Chart Room.

One fateful day, as I approached the Chart Room, three staffers were waiting to get in. One was Raylene, a physician's assistant and a favorite of mine for her colorful African kufi caps and the match- ing, psychedelic-patterned African gowns peeking beneath the hem of her white medical robe. I also liked her bright, toothy smile, rimmed by lips painted fuchsia or ruby red.

Thus far, it had been an especially aggravating day. At our treatment team meeting, all five vets, seen individually, had been edgy if not downright hostile: "I just got here, and you're already asking me about a discharge date?" "What do I wanna do with my life? I don't know!" Maybe their dark moods cast a spell on me.

"Don't you hate this waiting game?" I remarked outside the Chart Room. "Do you know how much I want to open that window and jump through?" I was joking, of course, but Raylene was looking for fun.

"I bet you could do it, with those skinny hips!" she said. "Go on, *sister*! Use those skinny hips!"

That was all it took. I was riled, and ready to make my move. In a leap of faith—and bad judgment—I slid open the window, hoisted myself up to the ledge and leapt through the window. Bing! My stilettos hit the tile floor, the clerks looked up—finally—and I opened the door to let in the people who had been patiently waiting.

Later that day, I received a voice message from an administrative assistant: "The Chief (of the Dom) wants to see you at 3:00 p.m. tomorrow."

This had to mean a reprimand: Conduct unbecoming of a social worker. In fact, I sensed something amiss right after my grand leap. The mood of my peers shifted, the joking stopped, my "friends" dispersed (without one "thank you") and the hallway grew suspiciously quiet.

Aha! I'd outed myself, I thought. The "real me"—the rebel, the daughter of a die-hard lefty—didn't fit into establishment culture (certainly not the federal government!), and probably never would, or could.

The next day, I waited outside the Chief's office, remembering the last time I'd waited, wracked with guilt, for disciplinary action. It was in high school, when my biology teacher sent me packing to the principal's office for a short skirt. This was during the mid-1960s. The rule was: If the skirt doesn't graze the knees, it's too short. Clearly, I was in violation by two if not three inches. The principal sent me home, and my mother lengthened the hem.

This situation was harder to fix. At the next day's dreaded Domiciliary meeting, the Chief of the Dom was very stern. High school revisited! She did not smile. She did not say hello. She sat behind a large desk in a tall, straight-backed chair. "I have several reports of contact," the Chief began, in a grave tone of voice, waving some baby-blue papers in my face. These were official forms reserved, specifically, for one staff person to write a complaint against another. She held three, written and dated by the very people for whom I had opened the door. She went on to explain "the disciplinary process," outlining "all possible outcomes of the case" (ranging from "a mark on your record" to "termination"). She mentioned the prerogative of the West LA VA Chief of Social Work—the Chief's boss!—to make a "final determination." This was the sternest language, and face, of VA officialdom.

She concluded the meeting with a warning, soft-spoken but firm: "You are going to have to live with this… Your colleagues expect you to act like a professional. It will take a long time to win them back."

I wanted to tell her: (1) that I didn't care; (2) that the fun-loving Raylene was technically guilty of sexual harassment for commenting on my "skinny hips"—a flimsy excuse to wriggle out of punishment, yes, and one I wouldn't dare use; and (3) that those clerks needed to do their jobs.

I didn't, of course, so the bureaucracy, like the flu, ran its torturous course as follows: email notification of a disciplinary hearing; another email informing me that "You are entitled to union representation" (Forget that—the union rep laughed when I called); and the meeting itself, whereupon I read my prepared statement, a wordy mea culpa, as if it were a speech of the Thirteenth Plenum of

the Executive Committee of the Communist International. Time
served giving boring address. That way, I figured, they'd let me off,
quickly.

But three months later, I was summoned to a third meeting
with the Chief, who announced that "the Social Work Department
has settled on a verbal warning," meaning, a slap on the wrist rather
than Alcatraz.

All this time, my family—unlike the VA staff—refused to take
the matter seriously. My husband's advice had been, "Cover your
mouth and try not to laugh... You know I'm proud of you!" while
my daughter, then just eighteen, mused, "I wish I could be like
that!" She reminded me of the time, six years before, I had thrown
off the lead apron at the dentist's office and walked out to protest
their insistence on the "full mouth" of x-rays I didn't need.

In the end, this silly little act of insurrection at the Chart Room
made me a star. Many in the rank-and-file applauded me, re-envi-
sioning and replaying the scene for weeks, as if it were "Mutiny on
the Bounty" and I was Brando. Few vets witnessed the crime, but
word traveled fast: Plate climbed through the window! In a skirt! A
command decision! A lady who gets things done! In their eyes, as
well as those of my colleagues, I had earned my stripes.

Today, it makes sense. Five years of government service had
pushed me to the edge (and over the ledge!), but with that one
wanton leap I made great personal strides. The wrath of the institution suddenly seemed less forbidding. And reckless silliness—maybe,
even, a little fun—wouldn't get me fired. In the end, with newfound
confidence and determination, I resolved to focus on helping veterans, not the crazy institution, and to soldier on.

Chapter Five

RISKY BUSINESS IN THE ERA OF HOPE AND CHANGE

The ghosts of Justin Bailey and Mark Torres lurked everywhere—at the lawn table, where veterans gossiped about the deaths, lowering their voices when staff walked by; at an emergency town hall meeting in the hospital, where a friend of the Bailey family stood before a microphone, reading aloud the names of the clinicians he held responsible for Bailey's death (I was exempt); on desks, where issues of the *LA Times* were neatly folded to keep the latest headlines hidden from view.

The two men were nothing alike—and yet both died, roughly one week apart, while under the care of the VA.

Justin

Surrounded by veterans twice his age, you couldn't miss this fresh-faced, twenty-seven-year old guy with thick, dark, hair; liquid brown eyes; and smooth cheeks. He was one of our first returnees from Iraq.

Then came Monday, January 29, 2007. News broke at the daily Domiciliary 8:00 a.m. staff briefing: "Patient A, discharged to family; patient B, room altercation with patient C, moved to room 245 East… *Patient Justin Bailey, expired.*"

Dead. Passed away. Found unresponsive by. Paramedics came. Unable to be resuscitated…

One name among many. A string of details. A horrible truth: Justin Bailey, one of the first Marines to enter Iraq, was dead.

He enlisted in 1998, just one month before turning eighteen, already with a history of marijuana and alcohol problems. He joined hoping that a few years in the Marines would set him straight. But after the terrorist attack on September 11, 2001, Justin's tour of duty was extended, and in 2003, on the eve of war, he was deployed to Iraq.

Returning home in 2004, Justin's alcohol and marijuana problems had gotten worse, compounded by the drastic effects of combat: post-traumatic stress disorder (PTSD), depression, a groin injury. The young man had trouble holding down a job, keeping up with rent, and maintaining relationships—common behavioral patterns attributable to PTSD. He was anxious. Hypervigilant. Insomniac. Plagued by intrusive thoughts. Paranoid. And more. The twenty-seven-year-old in fact told his mother, who would later tell the *LA Times*, that he was consumed by guilt over the deaths of innocent Iraqis: "I killed women and children. I can't deal with this." That comment, almost verbatim, would be echoed years later by many others who returned from Afghanistan and Iraq, but this "kid," as the Vietnam Era vets referred to him, was among the first.

By all accounts, the troubled young man didn't want to die, nor did he want to continue life as he had come to know it. So he decided to make his way from Las Vegas—his hometown—to the famed West LA VA, for treatment at the largest VA campus nationwide.

Immediately upon arrival, he was admitted to the psychiatric ward. Two weeks later, he was considered sufficiently stable for release. At that point, he was transferred to the Domiciliary for long-term residential treatment addressing problems of substance abuse and mental health.

On release from the psychiatric ward, he was taking a complex cocktail of prescribed medications: For pain, methadone. For depression and anxiety, bupropion (otherwise known as Wellbutrin) and Xanax. For insomnia, trazodone. For nightmares, prazosin. On January 25, 2007, he filled five prescriptions, including a two-week supply of methadone. The next day, he died. His grieving father told the *LA Times*: "They [the VA] gave him the bullet."

Mark

At fifty-three, Mark Torres had been abusing drugs longer than Justin Bailey had been alive. It showed. He wore a black patch over an empty eye socket resulting from a car accident. Every morning he stood in the methadone line—a tired-looking Hispanic guy, shoulders slumped, plaid flannel shirt slung over baggy jeans.

For thirty years, this veteran went in and out of programs for addiction to a smorgasbord of potentially lethal drugs: heroin, methadone, cocaine and benzodiazepines. For seventeen years, he went in and out of prison for drug-related crimes (forgery, failure to appear, parole violations, second-degree burglary).

Mark was a street guy, the type of vet we called a "frequent flier" or "repeat offender" (only to like-minded friends, of course). Unlike the young Bailey, he never faced combat. But for five years in the 1970s he, too, served in the Marines. Not surprisingly, this middle-aged veteran was chronically homeless, with multiple mental health diagnoses, including depression, mood disorder and psychotic disorder, the latter most likely due to drug abuse. In 2006, the courts delivered an ultimatum: return to treatment, or go to prison.

Of course, he chose treatment. Back in 2003, he had entered the Domiciliary, but left due to relapse on alcohol. So he chose to try something new: a program called New Directions, located on VA grounds but run by the Salvation Army. In therapeutic style, New Directions was less like the trendy, vet-friendly Domiciliary, and more like Dr. D's Recovery Treatment Center—that small pro-gram renowned for its rigidity and confrontational therapeutic style, where I began my social work career.

There was a hitch, though: New Directions prohibited patients from using methadone—even if it was medically administered and monitored. Staff subscribed to the old-school, hard-line view that if you take a mind-altering drug—any drug, even a prescribed opiate, even for the purpose of kicking heroin, even for a limited period of time, even under close medical supervision—you are not drug-free. You might as well get high, in fact! Zero tolerance meant absolutely no drugs or alcohol of any kind. Period.

To enter New Directions, then, the struggling veteran was forced to detox from both methadone and heroin. He had not done so in thirty years. As such, the plan was a set-up for failure. Within a month, he left New Directions, then applied for a second admission to the Domiciliary. There, the plan was to begin substance abuse treatment and resume a regimen of methadone maintenance. Unlike New Directions, our federal government/VA program accepted vet-erans engaged in methadone maintenance.

Unfortunately, the maintenance regimen couldn't begin over-night. First, Mark needed to undergo medical tests and assessments. Then the two clinics involved (the Dom, where the veteran was living, and the Opiate Treatment Program, which distributes meth-adone), would have to consult. It would take a few days.

In limbo, Mark waited—but developed intense cravings for heroin. He pleaded for help from Domiciliary nurses. It was Friday. His psychologist was out of the office but would be back on Monday. Soon after, he would begin methadone maintenance.

Alas, it must be said that recreational drugs are bought and sold on the grounds of the West LA VA. This may be shocking to out-siders, but it was common knowledge to those of us on the inside. Anyone can walk onto the campus and hang around. Sellers know where to find buyers. Mark Torres, a veteran of the streets, knew just whom to go to, and where, for a fix.

He died on February 2—one week after Justin Bailey. The coroner's report concluded that his death was "due to morphine (heroin) intoxication. Manner of death is an accident."

The Stage Is Set

One residential program, one week, two deaths. On your marks! Lights! Cameras! Action! Suddenly, people heretofore hidden within the bowels of the south side medical center rushed to the scene. Dr. E, a hotshot medical administrator, held an emergency meeting at the Domiciliary. He was an older, middle-aged, pale-faced Caucasian physician, utterly nondescript in appearance, now looking deeply anxious.

For the emergency meeting, business as usual ground to a halt. Classes were canceled. Patients milled around the quad smoking cigarettes, talking on cell phones, feeding squirrels inches from signs warning them not to do so (who was around to watch?). Said Dr. E, consoling us, if not himself: "The patients know why we are meeting and that we are concerned."

How did this happen, he asked? What had gone wrong? In the weeks to come, a slew of top-notch medical staffers echoed his cries.

Were they kidding? (Of course not!) They wanted an explanation for these tragic deaths? How many times, over the past year or two, had we social workers complained to our bosses at the Domiciliary: We can't cope with the overwhelming number of veterans! Please advocate for more staffing! These conditions are unsafe!

The sergeant/Assistant Chief of the Domiciliary shot back: "You think 70's a lot?? You're gonna get 100!"

Said the Gapper, that program coordinator who monitored the gaps between women's button-down blouses: "When I was in a social work position like yours, I had 100 patients, and I saw them all, every week."

I asked how she managed that: "With one eyeball per vet?" No, she didn't laugh at my feeble joke, but her audience did.

Let me be clear. We had no delusions of grandeur. We knew we couldn't prevent veteran overdoses or suicides. But we knew that with a ratio of 70 patients to 1 social worker—and the threat of that patient caseload mounting to 100—it would be impossible to meet standards of "due diligence." Stretched that thin, our best just wouldn't be good enough.

The head honchos should have known better. They should have listened. It was 2007—four years after the invasion of Iraq. That same year, an Army-funded study published in the *American Journal of Psychiatry* determined that nearly one in five combat veterans who had served in Iraq suffered from PTSD. This in turn correlates with substance abuse. In addition, these mentally disturbed men suffered physical pain, but the most effective pain medications—opiates—could be highly addictive. (And this was ten years before the opioid epidemic swept across America.) Who would monitor the distribution and use of these powerful drugs?

It took two dead veterans for these questions to be raised.

The Need to Know

If a tree falls in the forest and no one is around to hear, does it make a sound? If a veteran should die while in VA care and the media doesn't hear about it, does he die in vain?

A shrill alarm sounded, above the din and chaos created by the two veterans' deaths: Don't talk to the press! If anyone from the press approaches you, do not answer questions! All media requests must go through the VA Office of Public Affairs!

There was no period of mourning. No memorial services. No in-house weeping for the dead veterans. It was infuriating.

Shouldn't the press know? Shouldn't the public know?

Fortunately, I had enduring media ties, achieved through twenty-nine years of marriage to a workaholic journalist—including a six-year stint at the *LA Times*, years before. Despite massive staff cutbacks and firings at the newspaper, some of the old-timers were still there.

I called an editor and informed her of the two men's deaths. She was interested in the story.

Then a reporter called me. Several times, we spoke on the phone—background only, of course. There were simple ground rules: The newspaper would not use my name. No one would email me at the VA. All conversations would take place on my personal cell phone. In fact, my paranoia was so profound, to talk to them, every time, I drove off campus.

"Don't worry," the reporter said. "We're going into the story cold, through the parents."

On March 12, 2007, the *LA Times* ran the story: "Parents Blame VA in Fatal Overdose." It was entirely about Iraq War veteran Justin Bailey. Mark Torres, just another Vietnam veteran, didn't make news.

Then on April 4, 2007, another story ran in the *LA Times*: "Feds Investigating 5 Recent Deaths at West LA VA Hospital." (The additional three deaths were not at the Domiciliary, and were attributed to illicit drug overdoses as well as medical problems.)

Fortunately, the reporter kept her promise of confidentiality. And no one at the VA connected me to the two news reports.

RCA

The VA was abuzz. Two deaths meant two impending "RCAs." These are Root Cause Analyses, meaning, in-house VA investigations of "adverse events" (otherwise known as deaths). Unfortunately, and inexplicably, administrators had selected me to investigate the Torres case, maybe because I was new, I was diligent, I could write—and I didn't know how bad it would be. An RCA, also called a "root canal" for the pain it induces, is a thankless task. You have to review charts, conduct interviews and present findings to the top (now tarnished) brass. For me, that meant investigating my boss and my colleagues, who grew more desperate with each administrative pronouncement that, "No one is to blame." Plus, my "recommendations" for change would become mandates, and my colleagues were already overburdened.

I was lucky to have a great partner on this RCA—a star physician revered and loved by virtually everyone, with more than thirty years of VA service. Together, we read the autopsy and police reports. We interviewed eight to ten staffers who had crossed paths with the deceased. The good doctor interpreted the medical information (bottles by the bed; medications that were contraindicated). My task was to turn the findings into prose.

At first, we were treated well, with a temporary office in the inner sanctum of hospital administration; a Quality Assurance person on standby to assist; detailed instructions and hands-on help fitting our findings into a prefabricated RCA grid; good coffee in ceramic mugs, not styrofoam cups; and an infinite amount of time excused from our usual jobs. It was a bit much, and suspiciously so. Since when does the VA play nice with mid-level staff?

Things changed when we submitted our rough draft, which presented at least one clear finding: More services were needed for vets on methadone, so that men like Mark wouldn't be forced into either-or choices that could be deadly.

"This is not a root cause analysis!" said Dr. E, clearly annoyed. "We don't need all this stuff!" He explained that he wasn't interested in service gaps or staffing shortages—"It's not how many people you have, but how you use them." What he wanted to know, he said, was precisely "what happened on this day, at this hour, with this case."

That's all. The End. Then he circled a short paragraph: "These are your findings."

And so, our "independent" RCA was reduced to two bullet-points:

(1) Substance abuse assessments must be completed within a timely fashion (forty-eight hours after Dom admission); and

(2) Interdisciplinary treatment team meetings between staff and patients must take place within two weeks of admission.

Neither of these steps had been followed in the Torres case.

There was most certainly more to say. But my partner, the good doctor, a thirty-year VA survivor, knew better than to speak up; and I, a relative newcomer, followed her lead. So we forged on to a final draft, as per their instruction.

But I was not done. A month later, I told my boss, Chief of the Dom: "Don't ever ask me to do that again, or I will tell the truth." She complied.

The VA cannot handle the truth.

We Shall Overcome

No news was good news, but bad news had its advantages. The young dead man had made his mark. A year after his death, Congress passed the Justin Bailey Substance Abuse Disorders Prevention and Treatment Act, establishing standards of accountability for mental health services as well as prescription drug oversight. What did that mean? That the VA would be held accountable for patient safety. That vets couldn't hang loose in their bedrooms and manage their own potentially lethal medications. That administrators at all levels were scared, finally, and would have to take safety precautions. With wars overseas, you can't have veterans dying at home while in treatment at the Veterans Health Administration.

You could feel the fear, but you could also see its amazingly curative effects. Overnight, our individual social work caseloads dipped from seventy veterans to thirty. Magic! Now, I could remember the veterans' names—maybe, even, their stories—without checking computer notes to jog my memory as to who they were and what were their needs. Another hallowed change: A young, upstart psychiatrist was ushered into the Dom to oversee program safety. The new doctor, a hotshot from the University of California, Los Angeles (UCLA) was in his later thirties, but looked like the teen doc prodigy in that 1989–93 TV series "Doogie Howser." He had a lot of experience in substance abuse and a lot of ambition.

Almost immediately, the new doc established the SSMP, or Supervised Self-Medication and Management Program. This was a huge change! No longer could patients on narcotics manage their medications. Instead, Domiciliary pharmacists and nurses would dole them out, daily. No more stockpiling of lethal goods (oxycodone, morphine). No more vets trading prescriptions in order to get high.

In addition, admissions criteria for the program were made more stringent. Now highly unstable patients—those imminently suicidal or actively psychotic—were denied admission. A pre-screening committee was established to review patient charts and write "denials" for the highest of the high-risk patients—meaning, they wouldn't be granted interviews for admissions. Yes, deserving vets were turned away. In fact, the Dom barely opened its doors (although no one dared to admit that). For a while, patients deemed high risks for suicides or overdoses were not welcome... despite their desperate need for help.

We were traumatized. One more death would kill the program—and our spirits. We feared accepting any patient who mentioned suicide, thought about suicide, had a relative who had committed suicide… which eliminated more than 60% of all applicants each month. The inside joke was, "If we don't admit anyone, no one can die."

As a result, the patient count dipped to an all-time low (at one point, only half of the Dom beds were filled). Then calls poured in from referring clinicians at the VA's Mental Health Clinic, the West LA program for veterans with post-traumatic stress disorder and the medical wards, as well as from the two other VA hospitals further south, which lacked residential, long-term treatment programs: Loma Linda and Long Beach. They asked, and rightly so: Where can we send our patients? Why are you turning away people with the greatest need for treatment? Why can't we move patients into the Dom's empty beds?

Why? Because we had a singular goal: No more deaths. Ever.

Shaken, the VA poured its faith into the SRAPP (Suicide Risk Assessment and Prevention Policy). There was nothing new here. In fact, we had been using the SRAPP templates for years to determine a veteran's mental health stability. The computerized form consisted of a sixty-question checklist to be marked: "yes" or "no": "Family history of suicide?" "Have you ever attempted suicide, even if the attempt was aborted?" "Have you ever had a psychiatric hospitalization?" Et cetera.

It was hard to stuff a vet's life into those tiny checkboxes. The only place for description and analysis was a short paragraph at the end. Here you had to synthesize the one-word "yes" and "no" fragments into a coherent whole paragraph about: the patient's overall mental health; medical and psychiatric treatment needs; social support; substance abuse problems; and legal problems. Then came the end sentence with a one-word fill-in-the-blank: "This patient's risk for suicide is: High, medium, or low." Of note, hotshot Doogie Howser told me that anyone in the Dom had to be rated "low risk" (if moderate, he shouldn't be in the Domiciliary, because he might become suicidal and die).

But the age-old template came with a new mandate: Do these assessments much more frequently! (Protect the institution with a longer paper trail.) Now, we had to conduct suicide risk assessments at: Domiciliary screening interviews; Domiciliary admission, even if these two occur on the same day; within five days of admission, by a social worker; within five days to two weeks before admission, at the first interdisciplinary team meeting; every six weeks, at subsequent treatment team meetings; at the first sign of escalating depression; and on the day of discharge. *At least.*

Beleaguered veterans would say, "Do you *want* me to do it [commit suicide]?" or, "I didn't think about it until I came here!"

Pressed for time, staff took shortcuts by cutting and pasting previous assessments, or rearranging words here and there to avoid suspicion of doing so. It was a kind of "Don't ask, don't tell" policy. My own technique was to check the boxes as soon as the vet left my office, making informed guesses as to the answers.

I once asked a VA psychiatrist, "Do you worry all day about possible suicides?" She smiled and said something about "going with your gut." But that was precisely the problem. I didn't trust my gut.

Only once in my fourteen-and-a-half years of VA service did I dare to do so. This was in the case of Larry, a sixty-four-year-old Vietnam combat veteran who had lost two loved ones to suicide: his son, age twenty-six, and his younger brother. "You don't have to worry about me," he said, "because I know what suicide does to the people left behind." In addition, this veteran refused to take psychiatric medications since his son and brother were taking them at the time of their suicides. How unusual, for me—a depressed veteran refusing medications brought relief! Because he clearly didn't want to die and was willing, maybe, to suffer through, if not overcome, his pain.

True Confessions

Bad things happen to good people, and when you least expect them. One Friday afternoon, I was startled to see Lucy's face at the door. A staff psychologist, she was characteristically upbeat and relaxed—not your usual PhD. The daughter of a Holocaust survivor, she laughed a lot, since the VA was better than Auschwitz. But on this day, her expression was grim. "We have a situation," she explained, running through the scenario: A Domiciliary resident in our charge had confessed, in a private session with his trauma therapist, to selling heroin on VA grounds. He hid the drug inside his two prosthetic limbs. This presented three grave risks: (1) Selling heroin on VA grounds is a felony; (2) wracked with guilt and shame, the vet might become suicidal; and (3) he was a danger to his customers.

When the vet returned from the other VA clinic and came to Lucy's office, he looked wary and confused, but as we talked his eyes registered shock. "I'll never tell the truth again!" he screamed. "I'll kill myself!" He was a big guy with a booming voice, menacing even though wheelchair-bound. Harry, a veteran-turned-Dom Assistant, held him down. He continued to cry and shout. He was inconsolable. Finally, Lucy called the ER to request a psychiatric evaluation, I called the VA police to escort him to the ER, and DA Harry, as big as the vet, slipped into the backseat of the police car that arrived, alongside the veteran, for moral support. Would the psychiatric ward admit him? We didn't know, but at that point, we were done. Now a ward of the ER, he would be denied readmission to the Domiciliary due to his admitted crime. (The psychiatric ward did in fact admit him that Friday evening, but rumor had it that, ten days later, upon release, he resumed selling heroin.)

The Boy Next Door

We were lucky. That crisis was quickly resolved, but some episodes dragged on for weeks, and at those times your mind—or at least

mine—entertains all the worst-case scenarios, like suicide, homi-
cide, accidental overdose... That's how it was with Steven B, a
twenty-seven-year-old heroin addict already strung out for ten
years. This young man, father of a four-year-old son "somewhere,"
picked himself up from the corner of Hollywood and Vine one day
and stumbled into the VA. He looked like the proverbial boy-next-
door—reedy, boyish, with sandy-colored hair and blue eyes. But he
was an addict. His mother was also a heroin addict who had been
sober, though, for years. By the vet's account, his mom couldn't
abide anyone using heroin—especially her son (no telling where the
dad was). This was Steven's first effort at sobriety, he explained, so
his mother was proud that he sought help.

Alas, one month later, Steven relapsed. It was "just a small
amount," he said, plus "some marijuana." Nevertheless, the Domiciliary upheld a policy of zero tolerance—absolutely no drugs
allowed—so Steven would have to be discharged, as quickly as possible. Each hour that he remained with us put the program at risk.
Would he get loaded again? Would he overdose and die? I tried to
get him into other programs, but they all said "no" because of the
risk involved (which was, of course, precisely why he needed admission). Then, in a last-ditch effort, I pleaded with the Salvation Army
staff, who ran a shelter on VA grounds, to admit him as an interim
measure: "Please! I'm not 'dumping' him! I'll meet with him every
day!" They granted the vet a two-week stay.

I was still stressed. Where would he go after two weeks? What
if he overdosed again? The Boy Next Door and I formulated two
plans:

(1) Live with his mother and engage in outpatient
    treatment (but don't tell mom he'd actually relapsed,
    because she might refuse to take him back); and

(2) Follow the orders of the doctor at the Opiate
Treatment Program: Stay sober two weeks, then
apply for readmission to the Dom.

Crisis resolved.

That first weekend, Steven used again.

As written in the chart notes, he was found in a bathroom, glassy-eyed and weaving, syringes underfoot. He was discharged on the spot, with bus tokens and directions to a shelter, where he never showed up.

Surprisingly, the Boy Next Door answered his cell phone Monday morning. "I spent the night on the street," he said, "and I still want treatment." I wasn't so sure. His speech was slurred— not exactly a sign of motivation—but I had to take him at his word. Again, I consulted with the doctor at the Opiate Treatment Program. Given the patient's "spotty" history, he said, Steven could not start methadone until he was stably housed.

"You can't distribute such a powerful, tightly controlled drug to someone who is homeless," he explained. "He can't be counted on to leave the street every morning and come in for his daily dose. That has its own risks." He advised me instead to "see if he can manage independently for a few weeks, demonstrate commitment to sobriety, then try to get back in the Dom and start methadone." From the doctor's perspective, this made sense, but it was a classic social work Catch-22: Get the patient stable and sober, then get help.

The story ends here—not with a bang or a whimper, but with a disconnected cell phone and silence. Steven never again called or came back. I was disappointed, but not for long. By then I had become healthily anesthetized. I had learned to keep hope alive for the sake of the patient, even against great odds. But when the vet quit, I quit, too. As they say in the field: "Something is wrong if you're working harder than the patient." Actually, Steven *was* in fact working hard, as hard as he could, at the time; but at twenty-seven, it was too soon to face the prospect of a long life, drug-free.

Still, I felt some measure of satisfaction. No matter what happened to Steven in the future, I had done my best. I hadn't grown frustrated, and I hadn't given up on him. In addition, I had managed to protect myself, and the VA, from liability; this may sound cold and legalistic, but one too many patient safety casualties can shut a program down. In this case, though, we were home free. The patient's chart would say: Twenty-seven-year-old heroin addict, admitted to the Domiciliary; relapses in treatment; social worker finds him temporary placement on VA grounds; social worker meets with him daily to monitor mood, encourage treatment re-entry and devise a feasible treatment plan. Social worker follows up by phone. Vet vanishes.

That was all I could do. The rest was up to him.

Grave Matters

One of AA's tenets is that alcoholism is a family disease. I had many patients with the disease who had burned bridges to their families over many hard years of drug abuse, domestic violence, and time behind bars.

Except Jay H. He was different—a tall, slim, middle-aged black guy with a penchant for loafers and button-down shirts—"not a street guy," as he liked to point out. Jay had two young kids and a wife, but his marriage was unraveling, courtesy of crack cocaine, and his wife was having affairs. Jay came to the Dom knowing he'd done wrong, like a puppy kicked out of the house, hurt, whimpering and begging to be let back in.

One day in group, he told a story about the time he planned to bludgeon his wife to death: He invited her to a picnic, packing food, drinks, and a shovel. He dug her grave the night before in a remote part of the park. But on the day of her planned murder, he said, he "couldn't go through with it... I kept seeing her on the birthing bed." No one in group talked after that. No one wanted to mess with Jay.

At 8:15 the next morning, Jay knocked on my door. "I have to miss group," he said. "I'm going Christmas shopping with my wife." Did he really think I'd say yes? Was he requesting permission, or begging forgiveness? Jay, a savvy guy, read the look on my face and hit back: "I'm going whether or not you approve! She has the morning off work! It's the only time she can go! It's for my kids!! Their presents!" Never mind. He could rant all day. I would not be manipulated—Christmas! Kids! It was an all-too-familiar story: A vet disappears into drugs, abandons his family and then, years later, emerges as Father of the Year.

Unfortunately, kids provide good cover for drug abusers. They know that fatherly love can melt a social worker's heart, especially those who have young children. In one such case, a veteran presented an 8x10 framed photo of his darling baby girl to a thirty-something social worker, mother of two, and was granted permission to leave the program overnight. He did not return.

True to his word, Jay took off, and I panicked. What if he kills his wife? What if the shopping trip, like the picnic plan, ends in murder? A mall, Christmas, volatile emotions around the holidays!

And the Tarasoff Case! Did it apply here?

This was the landmark 1970s case, *Tarasoff v. the Board of Regents of the University of California*, which set the precedent for "duty to warn." What this means is, when a readily identifiable targeted person is in imminent danger, the therapist must breach the patient's confidentiality and warn the potential victim. I was pretty sure that Jay's case, on this day at this time, didn't justify a breach. He didn't say, "I'm going to kill my wife with a shovel today." In fact, he talked about Christmas shopping. What would I say to his wife? "Mrs. H, your husband planned to murder you some time ago but reneged on the plan?" Or, "Be careful shopping today! Avoid open ditches!" Still, I knew better than to make such a serious judgment independently, so I consulted with the Domiciliary psychiatrist. He in turn consulted with the Domiciliary Chief. The two then called the offices of VA regional counsel, which in turn telephoned a VA lawyer, then vacationing in another country, on the beach. Her verdict was swift: Mrs. H was not in imminent danger. The Beach Won the Case.

While the legal matter had been settled, my conscience had not. All evening I cased out the local TV news, listening for headlines like "Murder in a Mall" or "Next up: A Christmas Crime of Passion." That night, thoughts of the shovel kept me awake. How heavy a blow could knock her dead? How would he get her body into the makeshift grave? Why did I work with someone like this?

The following morning, Jay was back in group. For a second, I was relieved, but I dreaded telling him that he was going to be discharged. This was the consensus of everyone on staff who had run around in a frenzy the day before. Jay was judged too impulsive, too uncooperative, and too great a liability to be safely managed at this VA program.

"Let's face it, you love to control men!" Jay screamed to me when he heard the news. Of course! It's always the social worker who is blamed; because that's who manages the discharge, who essentially has to push the person out, who steps in to see the vet on his way out the door. And in this case, to be put out by a woman! Jay was so furious, he circulated a petition advocating his right to stay, but few patients signed. The situation resolved, however; Jay's wife invited him home. Lucky break. He was happy (and so was I).

A year later, Jay returned to treatment. He pulled me aside one day after group to "make amends," he said, using recovery-speak. "I know you were just doing your job." He went on to complete the program without incident.

Fortunately, Jay had buried the bad memories—his conflicts with me, his abrupt, forced departure from the program—and had not buried his wife.

Murderous Thoughts

Some patient threats were just talk, but you could never be sure. At the start of a discussion group one day, Geoffrey M, a middle-aged Navy veteran, asked: "If I threaten to kill you, can I stay in the program?" I had not seen this coming. This man was due to be discharged for fighting with a fellow veteran. But even as he said this, he was poised and calm, smiling faintly, hands folded in his lap. It was creepy. Still, it would have been best to ignore the remark and carry on—but then he called me a "racist." This accuser on the verge of discharge was African American, while the person with whom he had argued was white—and had been allowed to stay (he was not seen as the fight initiator).

In fact, Geoffrey's discharge wasn't only about the fight; it was about the fact that he loaned $100 to another veteran, despite the rule forbidding any exchange of money—in a hard-up patient community like this, cash exchanges can be dangerous. In fact, Geoffrey's buddy used it to buy drugs and did not return—so he'd effectively helped another veteran to relapse.

This was the only time I walked out on a group. "Racist" didn't bother me so much. Accusations like this were made all the time, to virtually all staff. I had been called anti-white (when denying program admission to a Caucasian veteran); anti-black (for any disciplinary action involving an African American); anti-male (as in the case of Jay); and anti-Jewish (for using the collective pronoun "they" when referring to Jews as a group; according to one vet, this was equivalent to regarding Jews as cattle).

Later that day, Geoffrey appealed his case to a new administrator, admitting that he had spoken publicly about his murderous thoughts but insisting that he didn't mean what he said. She was a young, very pretty African American woman, with a voluptuous figure and long dreads in her hair. She was also newly licensed and could be naïve, with a penchant for glossing over complexities that demanded further examination. She told me: "He says he was just speaking theoretically!" How did she know if that was true??

Geoffrey also appealed to the Chief of the Domiciliary, who called me in to review the case. At first, she asked about the two vets who had argued—"Are they black? Or white?"—then quickly caught herself: "Never mind, don't tell me!" But when I mentioned that the veteran about to be discharged was African American, she asked, "What's the race of the other guy?" Busted!

Many times, I argued with her that it was dumb to pretend the VA was race-blind.

By the end of the day, per her orders, both vets were discharged for fighting. Was this fair? No. The other guy didn't threaten my life. But administrators saw a problem: The one who talked about murder was African American. His opponent was Caucasian. In the name of alleged fairness—and legal liability—both had to go.

The Stalker

I have been threatened with arrest just once.

It had been a typically draining, exhausting day. Time for the comforts of home! But something happened: Backing out of the parking lot, my 1999 Benz bumped into a car in the row behind. It was such a light tap, I didn't know which car I had "hit." Raylene's red Cadillac? The white Ford pick-up? Neither was dented or scratched, so I drove home.

Yes, the right thing to do would have been to leave notes on both cars. That's the law. But this was a heck of a parking lot—the scene of drug deals, car windows bashed by angry veterans wielding baseball bats, and arrests of both patients and staff (the latter for domestic abuse). Given that history, the thought of leaving my name, phone number and address on two notes, in full view and within reach of everyone, was scary. I harkened back to that first day at the Recovery Treatment Center, when a co-worker shamed me for displaying a state license bearing my home address. Plus, no visible damage had been done to either car. No harm, no foul, right? I drove off, figuring a quick getaway was the easiest and safest course.

The next morning, pulling into the parking lot, a pack of guys were smoking in the quad, as usual; but suddenly, one broke away from the group and headed my way, quickly, giving the appearance of a fit of rage.

I was right. "We have to talk!" he said, as I locked my car. We stood there, face-to-face, no more than three inches apart. "You hit me and drove off last night!" he said. "Look what you did!" He stomped on his Ford truck's back bumper, with his boot, until it came loose and dangled by one end.

Obviously, this was a scam. No way my sedan, in reverse, going one mile per hour, could have crushed the back bumper of that Ford truck. Obviously the veteran saw dollar signs in my eyes, and on my Benz. He would fix his car at my expense. Somehow, I mustered up a scared, wobbly voiced "Call me in my office" and scurried off.

He called, alright—six times in the space of one hour. With each call his voice grew louder and more menacing: "What are you going to do about this? It's a big deal! You better give me your address and insurance info!" Each time there was a rant, then a click.

Later that day, the Domiciliary Chief called: "Did you know the police are here about a hit-and-run?"

I feigned nonchalance: "Send them down to see me," I said, shaken but pretty sure VA's finest would see the scam and come to my defense.

My office was small and dark, just wide enough for two pudgy cops to stand side by side, across from my desk, demanding to see my driver's license. How could I expose my home address to this furious, aggrieved Dom patient? "Ma'am, we can't discuss personal information on a veteran," answered one of the cops. What about personal safety? "Ma'am, it's the law," he said. And suppose this social worker doesn't comply? Said the second cop: "We will arrest you."

The time had come to call a lawyer/friend. "Get arrested, then released on your own recognizance five minutes later," he advised. This option held no appeal. Consider the gossip mill and the optics: Plate gets arrested by the VAPD. Plate is in custody…

No, now was the time to go by my gut: "If I hand over my driver's license to you and not the vet, would you take it upon yourselves to call the insurance company so that the 'other party' doesn't know where I live?"

They agreed to this plan. They probably didn't keep their word (why trust VA police?), but it felt better than being booked… even for five minutes.

About an hour later, my husband made a surprise visit to the VA for moral support. He looked dashing that day in his expensive, Italian pin-striped suit, red silk tie, and red silk pocket handkerchief. He strode in with his best Mafioso manner—heavy chin thrust forward, dark brows furrowed, lips set tight. (It was a look he had been practicing for years, since the New York subway ride following a wedding when some kids, impressed by his three-piece white suit, carnation and shiny black shoes, asked if he was in the Mafia.) Things are okay now, I reassured him, as we talked in that same parking lot.

But then, unexpectedly, both cops from earlier in the day rounded a corner of the Dom and headed our way. Now what?

"She's fine, sir," said the chattier cop, offering a handshake to my husband. "We always have to bend over backwards so that it looks like we're not favoring staff."

What did he think? That this man was my lawyer? A Mafioso? Both? No matter. They left, and my ersatz Don Corleone remained silent, as any true mafia man would.

Finally, 4:30 p.m. came around. End of the workday. Time to leave! Exhausted and spent, I was more than ready to slip through the glass doors to the parking lot and drive home.

But something unexpected happened, again—to my right, just as I opened the doors to the lot, there was a rustling in the bushes. Out popped the vet, like a jack-in-the-box. Obviously, he'd been lying in wait! What did he want? Hadn't the matter been resolved? Rattled, I made a quick bee-line to my car, locked the doors and revved up the engine.

Immediately, another engine started up. Whose? Coming from where? Backing up, looking in my rearview mirror, I saw the vet backing out, just like me. The whole scene had been perfectly timed.

A quick left onto the first street, Eisenhower Drive, leading to the main exit from VA grounds… The vet was still behind me. *Close* behind me. The large white hood of his Ford loomed in my rearview mirror, like a ghost, backlights flooding my car.

This, I couldn't handle. Working with veterans as patients, yes. But being followed? No. I made a fast U-turn on Eisenhower Drive, drove back onto VA grounds, past the Dom, a half-mile up the hill to the offices of the VAPD. Where was the vet? Had I lost him?

No matter. Spooked, I stepped out of the car, took the three stairs up the small, faded white wooden police headquarters and stepped inside to file a stalking report.

As it turned out, the VA cops did, finally, act on my behalf. They instructed the stalker not to speak to me, not to call me, and not to step onto the floor where I worked except for an appointment, in which case he was to leave immediately after.

Relief!

A few weeks later, the stalker was discharged from the Dom for abusing cocaine. No wonder he had been so excessively agitated, jumpy, aggressive... The speedy high of cocaine, not just anger, fueled those screaming, rapid-fire phone calls—all six of them within the space of an hour.

Not once did I suppose he was high. In social work, as in journalism, you lose your objectivity when you become part of the story.

What's more, the insurance company forwarded the case to fraudulent claims. What happened to the veteran? No idea, but I sure hoped he wouldn't come back. And my wish came true.

Danger Zone

We were in a gorgeous, split-level home overlooking LA. A kindly servant was making the rounds, kneeling before each guest with a silver platter bearing exotic hors d'oeuvres. There were four of us: the former foreign minister of a Southeast Asian country, his wife, my husband and me. That night, I played the role of Newsman's Wife. This foreign minister was a trusted journalistic source, one who offered good information and, on this night, a sumptuous Southeast Asian meal. Their daughter, age six, was somewhere off with her nanny.

"What kind of police presence do they have?" the foreign minister asked, curious about the Wife's job.

Good question. Shouldn't there be safety measures to protect staff working with patients who are severely mentally ill, addicted to drugs or alcohol and in trouble with the law? No, there are not.

"You mean these lunatics are running around free?" he asked.

Yes, they are. All day, every day (although I recommended dropping "lunatic" and replacing it with "disturbed"). I explained that you could call the VA police for help, but they were stationed in their own headquarters. No one stands guard at the Domiciliary or some of the smaller clinics. That would send the "wrong message," and only one (or two) were accepted as politically correct: "Welcome home" and "Thank you for your service."

Concerns about staff safety don't make for good politics. Accordingly, VA employees were forbidden to carry mace. Panic buttons were scarce. The Domiciliary was in fact allotted six, for well over one hundred employees. When the Chief asked who wanted one, no one spoke up—except me, asserting that we could not choose who should live and who should die. Clearly irritated, the Chief left, then distributed the six buttons to staffers on the medical floor. Meanwhile, the social workers and psychologists remained huddled together in the darkness of the basement floor (adjacent to the infamous parking lot!), panicked and de-buttoned.

My own habitat was the last office on the hall, nearest the parking lot. All day, veterans pounded on the double glass doors at the basement's west end. You never knew who it might be. Someone with a gun? Someone angry and bent on revenge? But it was actually stupid to worry. Most of these guys simply reached high and disconnected the electronic lock on top of the door.

"ER": Not Made for Prime-Time
The scariest place to work was the ER, across the way, on the north side of the VA. No, I was not hired to work there, but was required to do so a few times, as were all the licensed social workers. This was for reasons of cost. When the permanent hire for the 3:30 to 11:30 p.m. shift was absent, a rotating schedule for substitute ER social work coverage was established. Thus, there were times I would report to my job at 8:00 a.m., get a voicemail message: "You are needed in the ER," then drop my work at 3:00 p.m., cancel all groups and appointments, drop all cases and drive to the hospital... for another eight-hour shift. Surely a sixteen-hour workday was a labor violation (or is the federal government exempt?) Our union's

response was, "Nurses do this all the time!" We balked. We whined. We threatened to resist, but did not. Nothing changed.

And so, the first words I heard, my first time on call were: "This is the toughest case you'll get here." The outgoing day-shift social worker gave me the rundown of what lay ahead: "Vet, a returnee from Iraq; age twenty-two; severely alcoholic; multiple recent drug- and alcohol-induced episodes of violence in the ER; assaultive; aggressive; two days ago, trashed the Christmas tree in the lobby. ER doctors are fed up and want him out. I have never seen a doctor-social worker fight this brazen." Lucky me.

It's a common scenario. Doctors, eager to move the bodies, insist on discharge from the psych ward and refuse to approve one more overnight stay, despite the social worker's objections that discharge on such short notice could be unsafe.

I arrived in fear. We'd all heard plenty of ER horror stories, like the one about the MD who burst through the doors yelling, "Chaplain! I need a chaplain!" and the social worker who ran off yelling same. When you don't know what you are doing in an area like this, it all feels like a crisis. Where's the scotch tape? How do I work the "pool" beeper? The VA wouldn't pay to supply beepers to each nightly substitute; they paid instead for one, which was turned over to whoever was on call that night. No time for fumbling or an accidental disconnect.

A nurse led me to the black-and-white wall monitors by which staff kept watch over psychiatric patients in lockdown. "Here's your guy," she said with a smile. "My guy?!" All you could see was a blanket, outlines of a body underneath lolling from side to side, arms and legs twitching in a state of acute alcohol detox. "We'll call you when we know what's going to happen with him," she said.

For an hour-and-a-half, I panicked. What do I do with this guy? Where can I send him? Do I see him by myself, given his violent history? Will he spit at me? Take a swing at me?

The suspense was intense, so an hour-and-a-half later I located that nurse and requested an update. Oh, she forgot to tell me—the situation had been resolved. A senior social work supervisor had been called in to mediate the doctor-social worker stand-off. The doctors had been ordered to cease and desist: "This is a twenty-two-year-old returnee from Iraq!" said the supervisor. "We have nowhere safe for him tonight!" He would be discharged the next morning.

Fortunately, the rest of the night was quiet, so I hid behind a computer at my "work station," situated in the central nervous system of the ER, with resident MDs seated to my left and right—one who looked like a Ken doll in scrubs, the other an Asian kid with spikey hair. Both looked like they had just left band practice in their garages.

In fact, many ER doctors were the enemy of the social workers. They were arrogant and authoritarian. They would tell you to "Move him out" (of the hospital) and dismiss your objections with statements like "Read the chart notes, you'll see that he has to go" (of course, I already had) and "He doesn't mean it when he says he's going to commit suicide."

Okay, are you willing to put that in the record?

I didn't think so.

Worse, the MDs knew nothing about housing resources. One night, the on-call doctor stopped at my doorway to say just one thing: "Social work?" I nodded. He then requested that I "find something" for a veteran needing an overnight stay so as to be on time for an early morning eye appointment. When I mentioned transitional housing programs, he laughed because "he's not that kind of guy." I offered to accompany the good doctor for a visit to "that kind of guy" in one of the ER exam rooms. He happily agreed. But about a minute into the three-way dialogue, literally behind my back, the good doctor slipped out of the room. The veteran continued to vent, and continued to refuse any temporary housing options besides an upscale hotel room. A few minutes later, I left him, mid-rant. The MD who had sneaked out stood in the center of the ER, already bent over another patient's chart.

A month later, I was again summoned to the ER. This time, I had an "office"—a tiny, dark, windowless space situated at the end of a long, dark hallway, with the patient waiting area just one door away. Flora, the social work supervisor, gave me an intensely grave orientation: "After 6:00 p.m., when the day staff has gone, lock the door of the hallway. Also, lock the door of your office, even when you are inside. Any time you exit the office, turn off the lights so they think no one is in there. Pull your car into the space closest to the ER entrance so you can get there quickly at 11:30 p.m." Then, with a wink and a sadistic smile, she said, "You do know, don't you, that patients wander."

Compared to other hospital ERs, the VA's is unique. A lot more drama goes on than tending to heart attacks or car crash victims. In effect, this ER also serves as an after-hours homeless center—a free-for-all for veterans straggling in from the streets. They come seeking beds, psychiatric evaluations, and above all, bus tokens, which aren't available anywhere else after 4:30 p.m.—in LA, with no efficient, wide-ranging subway or train system! Veterans also come hoping for taxi vouchers to take them somewhere to sleep for the night. Others request tokens after they've been seen and discharged from the ER.

Deciding which means of transport to give, to whom, isn't as easy as it might sound. You could endanger a patient's safety by underestimating his disability and putting him on a bus. Or you could be accused of wasting government funds by putting him in a taxi when he might just as well have taken the bus. I once mis-counted the vouchers and gave some lucky vet the equivalent of one hundred dollars' worth of vouchers (rather than ten). He must have partied hard that night.

At the end of my shift, 11:30 p.m., I crept quickly through the dark, foggy air to my car. The lot was almost empty. All those cars I'd seen when entering at 3:00 p.m. had been driven home. Fortunately, no one drugged and desperate was waiting outside.

The Angel of Death

The ER preached strict fiscal conservatism. I first realized this when handing bus tokens to a man in a wheelchair. Flora, the ER supervisor, sneaked up on me from behind. I nicknamed her The Angel of Death, for a few reasons.

First, Flora always wore black. All black. All day. Every day. Not a hint of color, even on her shoes. Maybe she was aiming for a slimming effect. She was indeed chubby, and with that silver-toned pixie haircut, she had a gnomish look.

Second, she was a nitpicking, nervous Nellie, prone to poking her upturned nose into everyone's business. Did you document this? Did you check on that? Make sure you carry the beeper at all times!

That evening, as I started to hand over bus tokens to a wheelchair-bound man, Flora swooped in like a fighter pilot to declare, "We don't give bus tokens!"

I was confused. Sure, we do! We always do! The poor veteran's hand was suspended in mid-air. Flora then yanked my elbow, pulled me into "my" tiny, dark office, shut the door and scolded: "We can't have these kinds of conversations in front of veterans! Is he indigent? Have you done an assessment?" For bus tokens?? I did not speak. The beeper was beeping (doctors calling from the medical wards), and the phone was ringing (nurses in the ER signaling that someone in an emergency bed needed… something). And where were the scissors? Tearing open a fresh packet of bus tokens with my teeth, I pulled out a few and returned to the veteran, still sitting patiently, and placed the tokens in the palm of his hand. It closed instantly, like a flower at sunset.

The rest of my tour was quiet, except for the patient discharged from a medical ward late in the day who refused to go to a shelter; refused to go anywhere in downtown LA; stated that he had no more than $40 in cash; and admitted that he had not taken his medications for bipolar disorder. "Put me up in a hotel," he said. Obviously, he was new to the VA, so I apologized and explained that we weren't able to offer that. The vet flipped me off, yelling "Forget it! I'll sleep in my car!" then walked away. How I had changed! What once seemed unthinkable—a veteran sleeping in his car— now seemed like a decent interim "housing" option.

The next morning, back at the Dom, Flora called, sounding panicked. I braced myself. What would she say? That someone I allegedly helped at the ER had died? Fallen off a bus and been hospitalized? Complained to his Congressman that I wouldn't give him money to pay for a hotel?

"We were missing three bus tokens!" she gasped. "But I found one on the floor. Where are the other two?"

It was 8:15 a.m. Nine hours ago I had put in a sixteen-hour workday, under considerable duress, with patients who were acutely disturbed, scurrying up and down a dark, half-deserted hallway. After all that, she's hounding me about two bus tokens?! For the sum total of what, maybe, two dollars?! In a flurry of nerves, Flora hung up without my answer.

A few hours later, she called back with an update: One token had been found on the floor, but the other was still "outstanding." That's when I made two offers: (1) Reimburse her for the cost of the missing token; or (2) Write her a check for $500 if she would promise not to call again.

With that, I figured I'd be banned from the ER.

Alas, no such luck. I had done my best, and Flora knew it. No one on my watch had died. Such was the inevitable bottom-line. In her heart—and I knew she had one, beneath the layers of black clothes—Flora knew she could count on me to stay steady, even amidst the chaos of this rather unusual homeless access center/emergency room.

I don't know whether she found the last missing bus token. Maybe, because she didn't call back.

Chapter Six

A NEW BREED OF
WOUNDED WARRIORS

We were having dinner in a high-end home on a small suburban street south of Saigon (Ho Chi Minh City).

"The war was thirty-two years ago. What troubles them so?"

She was slim and elegantly dressed, this high-ranking Vietnamese ambassador to the European Union—a teenager when Americans bombed her hometown of Hue.

Typically, I explained, PTSD surfaces years after the trauma.

Then the dinner host, a Vietnamese media and government representative, asked, "Why don't our soldiers have PTSD?"

"Perhaps because you don't diagnose it."

And that was before the main course.

American Sniper

A new generation of vets clashed with old treatment models. Anthony M, age twenty-five, was a star sniper who had served in Iraq, Afghanistan and Saudi Arabia. Like the late Chris Kyle of "American Sniper" fame, Anthony was revered for his many "kills." His friends called him a "master" at blowing off people's heads. Anthony had done prison time for beating his wife when he caught her cheating. Among other things, he broke her nose. He had also done prison time for beating up the ex-boyfriend with whom she cheated. The victim sustained permanent brain damage, but Anthony showed no remorse. "It's the Marine thing," he explained, with a soft smile and a shrug. His drug of choice was Valium—he claimed to have swallowed forty at a time, but insisted, "I didn't want to die. I just wanted to calm myself." At least once in the past he had pointed a gun to his head but failed to pull the trigger because of his kids, whom he vowed to "rescue from foster care" (evidently, his wife had problems of her own). The law prohibited Anthony from carrying a firearm, of course, but he nevertheless took his girlfriend on a date to a rifle range, which ended in his arrest. What do you call a guy like that? A daredevil? A sociopath? A severely damaged veteran?

Anthony was court-ordered to treatment. He did well at the Domiciliary, but then got in trouble for violating four rules: (1) having a woman in his room; (2) possessing marijuana on government grounds; (3) consuming that marijuana on government grounds; and (4) doing so in his room, which posed a fire hazard. He was discharged, but this star sniper had political pull. His advocate complained to authorities in D.C., who then demanded his readmission, so the psychologist who had discharged him called to invite him back. He accepted the offer.

Why such special treatment? If you want to keep a war going, you can't have veterans wandering the streets. Yes, this is unfair, but the vets of the Vietnam Era had already been written off as lost causes. For the ongoing wars, the government still had hope.

Tailored to War

The first years of the Iraq War, the VA's approach was "one size fits all." Veterans of every age, race and gender swam together in one big patient pool. Inevitably, the older, Vietnam Era vets bumped elbows with "the kids," whom they resented for being moved to the head of the line for appointments and individual counseling at the behest of the federal government. Who doesn't suffer fear and humiliation at the thought of the younger generation nipping at their heels?

The message was clear: With America engaged in two ongoing wars, those who recently served get preferential treatment. For
patients like Anthony, a computer pop-up reared its head as soon
as you typed in the name: "This is an OEF (Operation Enduring
Freedom, from Afghanistan) or OIF (Operation Iraqi Freedom)
veteran... Should be given priority..." Friction between young and
old warriors became a hot topic of discussion in therapy groups. I
remember one in particular. We got to talking about differences
between wars: hand-to-hand combat versus drones; popularly supported wars versus the debacle of Vietnam; the forgotten generation
versus the new kids on the block. Sensing the group's mood, a young
returnee broke in quietly, to say: "You guys paved the way for people
like me." It was a transcendent moment. But it was Justin Bailey
speaking, four days before he died.

As more troops came home, changes were in order, particularly in the area of substance abuse. The abstinence model was seen
as old-school. How do you tell a twenty-two-year-old that he can't
have a drink, snort or puff—ever again, in his life? (Would you tell
that to a college student?!)? The Twelve Steps were no longer touted
as the sole path to a sober future. These young returnees, cynical if
not cocky, didn't believe in a Higher Power or God; as persuasive
counter-evidence, they referenced the carnage of war. Some went to
alternative self-help groups like Rational Recovery (AA for atheists)
or SOS (Secular Organizations for Sobriety).

Even the popular, evidence-based, universally acclaimed
"Matrix" model for substance abuse treatment, embraced by the
U.S. federal government, was called into question. Matrix is a smorgasbord of therapies: cognitive behavioral therapy (how to change
behavior by reversing negative thoughts into positive ones); self-help
(AA-style philosophy); and psychoeducation (on the adverse effects
that drugs have on the body and the brain).

Still, the overarching theme of Matrix is: abstinence.

Do No Harm

Enter a new treatment model: "Harm Reduction." As stated by the National Institute of Health: "When applied to substance abuse, harm reduction accepts that a continuing level of drug use (both licit and illicit) in society is inevitable and defines objectives as reducing adverse consequences. It emphasizes the measurement of health, social and economic outcomes, as opposed to the measurement of drug consumption."

In practice, this meant promoting risk reduction—strategies like "safe coping skills," motivational interviewing and cognitive behavioral techniques—rather than full-on abstinence. Forget that! For some, the end goal was to avoid driving while under the influence, or to quit drinking on the job. In truth, methadone maintenance was an early form of harm reduction; although it is an opiate, methadone is safer and less addictive than heroin, so patients who take it daily can lead productive lives. Another example of harm reduction: needle exchange programs.

But how do you define harm? What are the limits to approved use? Questions like these were particularly pertinent to the young men suffering from combat trauma. Obviously, marijuana is less harmful than crack or meth, so habitual use seems like no big deal. But if a veteran knows that zero tolerance is no longer the rule, why not smoke whenever he wants? Many in fact contended that PTSD, not alcohol or drugs, was their problem: "I didn't have a drug problem before the Service," they'd say, pointing out that Afghanistan is the opiate capital of the world. Said one vet with a rueful smile: "Ah, the poppy fields…" He also mentioned a whole lot of hashish and of course, alcohol, which is inevitably part of military buddy culture. Nevertheless, conventional wisdom is that both disorders—substance abuse and mental illness—should be treated simultaneously.

But what about the older veterans? Meanwhile, on other Domiciliary treatment teams situated on other floors—but in the same two buildings—the abstinence rule held. Imagine the complaints: "I have to be totally sober, when I can smell alcohol on these kids in the elevator? They're bouncing into walls and I can't have one drink?" To old-school, well-established addiction therapists, harm reduction was heresy. They had a point. How did it differ from recreational use? Answer: It didn't, except for the end-goal: To use with some discretion—and restraint—so as to curtail catastrophic consequences.

Harm reduction was a hard-sell. When a veteran failed to submit to a mandatory Monday UA (urinalysis test), the old guard would protest that "no test is a 'dirty test'! Discharge!" The counter-argument was: Are we going to take a guy in his early twenties, one or two months back from war, who may have PTSD and/or TBI (traumatic brain injury from bomb blasts), and discharge him for missing one test in his first few weeks of residential care? It was a winning argument. VA authorities in Washington wanted these veterans *off the streets*. We were ordered to keep them in residential treatment—even, at times, when they repeatedly relapsed. The goal was to reduce harm not just to the veterans, but to the VA's public image.

Chaos resulted. Hiromi, a twenty-five-year-old Japanese-American, was severely addicted to marijuana. Five times in less than five months, he relapsed. Five times the Chief told me that "they" (the D.C. desperadoes in politics and public relations) "want you to work with him." Meaning, no discharge. No referral to another program. "They don't see the point of pushing him from one homeless program to another," she said. "They want him to finish treatment and be housed."

They had a point; but how do you keep people sober, with absolutely no negative consequence for relapse, I asked?

Lucky for the Chief, the phone rang.

New Practices and Policies for New Veterans

All rules and regulations must be reviewed, and reviewed again, through the lens of new wars. Thus, the short-term, ninety-day stay in treatment under the Bush administration was greatly extended, sometimes up to a year, under President Obama. The theory was that more time in therapy would result in better outcomes (less homeless).

Psychiatrists had to adjust medications. Anxiety and depression are effectively treated with anti-depressants and anti-anxiety medications (Zoloft, Prozac and the like, as advertised on TV). But some of the young guys refused to take them for fear of sexual dysfunction.

"I'd rather be anxious than impotent," they would say, or, "If I can't have sex I'll be even more depressed."

Vocational rehabilitation specialists had to envision a new working order. Old-school theory held that the newly sober should focus exclusively on substance abuse treatment, even for a year, until stabilized, because they are "not ready" to face the stresses of work. The risk for relapse is too high.

But the federal government had a different concern: producing statistics that prove America's warriors had ample work opportunities back home. Therefore, jobs—and veterans getting them—became a paramount concern. This resulted in a short-cut, from treatment to employment, much favored by young, impatient men eager to make up for "lost" civilian time. They envisioned this speedy trajectory: Get a little treatment, or at least dry out; get a job; get income; get a place to live; and get back your wife and kids.

Marvin J, age twenty-six, was a case in point. He didn't need substance abuse treatment, he said; he binge-drank only on weekends. He was happily immersed in studies at a community college. He felt motivated. He had hope. But the program rule was, all new admits are restricted to VA grounds for thirty days. Forced to choose, Marvin opted out of treatment. A few months later, the program adopted a more holistic view, and Marvin would have been granted a recovery program tailored to his needs.

Did we lose him? Did he crash and burn in school? Perhaps. I don't remember him coming back. Many in that first wave of returnees quit substance abuse and mental health treatment to pursue education and employment.

Veterans like Marvin have a dream: To be an educated professional—some kind, any kind—whether in banking or physical therapy. But VA vocational rehabilitation specialists, many of whom were paraprofessionals and former patients, towed a different line: Get a job. *Any* job. Stay off the streets. Be humble. Start at the bottom.

Can drudgery become a dream? It wouldn't seem so. Not in America. Not anywhere, including the country of Malaysia. Back in 2009, in the *International Journal of Psychosocial Rehabilitation*, a Malaysian expert wrote: "Based on the importance of viable employment in the rehabilitation of the client who abuses drugs, the vocational training… needs to change. Specifically, training as computer programmers or electronic technicians may provide a better incentive then rattan making for inmates to remain drug free upon their discharge." So there, tough-talking professionals!

In virtually all ways, when the OIF/OEF vets came home, business as usual came to a dead-end. At my place of work, the longstanding policy of bed checks and head counts came under fire. For many years, there were bed checks twice-nightly, around 11:00 p.m. and 2:00 a.m. At these times, an army of Dom Assistants made their rounds, knocking on veterans' doors; entering with flashlights; conducting body counts (these were two- to three-men rooms); and reporting their findings to staff the next morning.

For combat veterans with PTSD, all this was intrusive and traumatic. Already hyper-anxious and easily startled, sudden flashes of light revived memories of bomb blasts. Quick, intrusive movements reminded them of ambush. Vietnam vets had been saying this since the 1970s, to no avail; but the young guys simply wouldn't have it, and the VA was forced to take heed. Some patients demanded the bed closest to the door, in order see the person entering rather than be suddenly awakened, in fear. In addition, the Dom Assistants were ordered to knock more loudly and enter more gracefully.

You had to be cautious around a sleeping veteran. Never touch him. Never get too close. If suffering from severe PTSD, bipolar disorder, or schizophrenia, he might become violent when aroused. For example, consider the female Domiciliary Assistant who happened to be Muslim. Stationed on the combat trauma floor, she wore a hijab. The psychologist in charge had pleaded that the woman be transferred to another floor on grounds that her presence induced the veterans' paranoia and generalized fear. The psychologist was told, "We can't discriminate against workers on grounds of religion," and, "Would you prohibit the Jewish MD from wearing his yarmulke?" In other words, the VA didn't dare risk transgressing a staffer's religious rights in the name of patient care.

One fateful night, a startled, disoriented young vet, aroused from sleep during a bed check, lunged forward and attempted to strangle the Muslim worker. She managed to free herself, but finally, the next day, she was moved off the floor. Now everyone was happier—the veterans, no longer having to see her hijab; the administrators, no longer vulnerable to a lawsuit on grounds of religious discrimination toward an employee; and the hijab-wearing employee herself, who had proven her might, and right, by wearing religious dress to work, and, in so-doing, out-ranking the veterans.

Even *Playboy* magazine became a topic of dispute. During a routine room inspection, Dom Assistants found a stash of them wedged under a loose ceiling tile propped open with a raisin box. These old-schoolers argued that pornography, like alcohol, was

prohibited on government grounds, and that possession was a pun-
ishable offense. They said this to me, because it was my patient on
my floor who had committed this alleged federal offense.

But I let it go (and they were furious). The gentleman in question was an Iraq returnee. He deserved his *Playboy*, or so I thought.
Imagine the negative news reports were he discharged! But the Dom
Assistants demanded equal rights for all veterans, of all wars, at all
times, even in matters of sex and pornography.

They could not understand nuanced care. One evening, a Dom
Assistant making the rounds discovered an elderly Vietnam veteran
in his wheelchair, being treated to oral sex by a woman of lesser
repute—in the Domiciliary chapel, which was open all night for
"prayer." The Assistant refused to interrupt. (And why should he?
The rule was, no female in your room, but common areas, like the
chapel, were *not* off-limits) The DA's underlying message was clear:
Sexual permissiveness for all, whether young or old.

Ladies Last

In the early years of the Iraq War, female veterans slowly trickled in.
They, too, were thrust into the general patient pool. Sometimes we
had fifty-seven male residents and three females on the same floor.
Of course, the women complained that they were "hit on." And
they were scared—because their doors had no locks. The open-door
policy had been in place for decades, to ensure staff access to all
rooms in case of emergency.

Women have served in all of America's wars, but the Veterans
Administration did not serve them until the 1980s. Accordingly,
when they first arrived at the Dom, we were not prepared. All UAs
(urinalysis tests for drugs) for veterans, both male and female, were
observed by males on staff. Men observed male patients standing
close by, inside the bathroom; they observed female patients from
the doorway, facing away, in the direction of the hall.

This practice was not questioned. In fact, once, needing a man on staff to monitor a urinalysis test for a patient who seemed under the influence, the Assistant Chief—Jean, or Ms. Carter, or Sergeant—barked at me: "You can do it yourself! We don't discriminate!" Fortunately, an administrator pulled the tough-talking sergeant aside to explain the ethical and therapeutic ramifications of that:

(1) A female social worker or psychologist cannot watch a man urinate into a cup if she engages him in individual therapy, listens to his deepest confessions, and, as is often the case in individual therapy, becomes the object of his intimate fantasies;

(2) Some of these men have been sexually victimized by women, including their mothers; and

(3) Observations by the opposite sex would open the door to allegations of sexual abuse.

Fortunately, visiting higher-ups issued an immediate ban on the practice of male staffers observing female patients. From then on, only female Domiciliary Assistants (of which there were few) had permission to observe female patients (not too many of those, either, thankfully).

In time, women got their own locks, their own rooms, their own floor at the Domiciliary and their own (female-specific) treatment program. Sexual trauma is a well-known hazard of military service. It had been making news since the Tailhook scandal of 1991, when more than a hundred Navy and Marine officers assaulted or harassed female officers at the Las Vegas Hilton Hotel. Now, with an all-volunteer military and increasing opportunities for women, staff was directed to trainings on the topic of MST (military sexual trauma) as well as other female-specific treatment needs.

Reverse Discrimination

There were a lot of wrongs to be righted, and the VA tried to do so all at once, with ferocity. Patient Mary J, for example, came to the program before the implementation of a separate women's track. The vets nicknamed her "Janis Joplin" for her long, straggly blonde hair, ripped jeans and roughhouse ways. One day, she voiced several complaints about "Mr. B"—a thirty-something, African American veteran who happened to be on my substance abuse treatment team. She said he was "looking at me funny," and she objected to his tone and manner when he said, "You look nice." This single perceived offense, which Mary mentioned to several on staff, launched a cannonade of phone calls my way: from the women's outpatient clinic at the main hospital; the woman's Domiciliary psychologist; and the Chief of the Dom, who summoned me to her office to ask, "Did you speak to the victim first?" No, I explained, defending my decision: "I spoke to my patient (Mr. B), first. He's the one with whom I have a therapeutic rapport. I'm not even sure she was a 'victim.'" This approach was unacceptable, she said. "Always go to the accuser first!" (Would that apply if the accuser were male?)

From then on I advised my male patients: "Stay away from the women. Don't talk to them. Don't say hi."

One male veteran asked: "When a female smokes a cigarette in the quad, braless, in a sheer blouse, in the freezing cold, am I not supposed to look?" He argued that some of these women, already "messed up" by their military trauma, were actually trolling for sex (then cried foul, maybe to get attention). Nevertheless, I advised: Don't look.

It was not an egalitarian culture. It was not a gender-neutral culture. When the laundry machines on the women's hall broke down, female veterans were permitted to use those on the men's floor, anytime, unannounced; but when the second-floor washers on the men's floor broke down, male veterans were denied entry to the women's floor without staff escort. The men complained, so I told the Chief of the Domiciliary. Her answer: "You can tell them that's because of thousands of years of oppression!"

Another example: Women, but not men, were routinely granted weekend passes to go off grounds. When questioned, the Chief said, "They have children!"

And men don't??

Now the male veterans' rights were at risk.

Sex Education

Something was wrong. I could sense it, and see it, the moment I returned to work Monday morning when a group of veterans seemed very upset. How was their weekend?

"Lousy!"

Something wrong?

"You bet!"

Unbeknownst to me, a directive had been issued Friday afternoon that all male veterans were to be "educated" on the topic of sexual harassment. Audrey was assigned to speak to the guys on my floor. She was a "lifer"—the term for those whose only employer was the VA. She had in fact started there more than twenty years before, in a low-level clerical job. Now she was supervisor of the Dom Assistants. Audrey cut an imposing figure. At 5'11", not counting the four-inch stilettoes, the vets described her as "ghetto chic," "hard-ass" or "the African queen." This Monday morning, they vented at what she had "taught" them:

(1) Never look a woman directly in the eyes, because that's intrusive; focus instead on her forehead; and

(2) Never let a woman know you're staring at her from behind. (Audrey told them, "I know when I walk out of this room you're all staring at my ass.")

What did I think, the guys asked? On the contrary, I said, the eyes are the windows to the soul, so look deeply within. When asked if I, too, felt the heat of their eyes "from behind," I made fun of myself, as I knew they saw me—a skinny uptown girl with a boney butt.

Caution! Transgender Veterans Crossing

In the early Obama years, the rights of transgender persons to serve in the military wasn't even a hot topic on cable news, or in class-rooms and living rooms.

Thus, we were not prepared for Ella Lee, a forty-something veteran transitioning from male to female. She was flighty and out-wardly girlie, with peroxided hair, a heavily pancaked face and a penchant for floral print, diaphanous dresses. A free spirit, she was prone to cartwheeling down the hall and blowing bubbles during groups on stress management. Anatomically, however, she remained male; her surgery was not yet complete.

Where to house her? First, she was placed on a men's floor, but soon after she complained that the men were "coming onto me." And yet, they couldn't place her on a women's floor. This had been tried a year earlier, with another male-to-female transgender vet-eran, and resulted in a legal judgment against the VA. In that case, a female roommate, a survivor of military sexual trauma (MST), claimed she was re-traumatized one night upon awakening to see her transgender roommate in the bathroom, genitalia exposed.

Administrators were so desperate, they considered housing Ella on the "cancer" floor. She did not have cancer but the unspo-ken assumption, or hope, was that these ill veterans wouldn't have the wherewithal to bother her. Then a nurse practitioner strongly objected: "Those cancer patients need peace and quiet, not the belle of the ball!"

Eventually, Ella got a single room. Problem solved.

I didn't know Ella, but I loved J-Hi, also a male-to-female transgender veteran. Her birth name was distinctly masculine— something like Bill Hughes—which was still the name on her patient record. Three times she came to the Domiciliary, tired of homelessness and turning tricks.

The first time she looked predominantly male, dressed in black leather pants, a colorful print bandana and two over-sized silver hoops dangling from her ears. I remember seeing her for the first time, in a heated argument, snarling and stomping away from some macho guys. A short time later, she tested positive for crack and left the Domiciliary program.

I saw her again about a half-year later, waiting to be interviewed for Domiciliary admission. This time she wore a shoulder-length, blonde wig and a baby-blue spaghetti-strap dress, despite the chill of winter. Again, she left the program shortly after coming in.

The third time was the charm—for me, and for J-Hi. She got her own room on a men's floor (mine). This time, her appearance was far more feminine. She wore dresses every day, wigs in a variety of styles (tousled red tresses; a chic, black bob), and always a velvet ribbon choker, she explained, "to hide my Adam's apple." But her sexual reassignment surgery had been stopped. With an enlarged heart from abusing crack, she was prohibited from further surgeries until she stayed sober, which is what brought her back for treatment.

This girl had moxie. Three mornings a week she strode proudly, if not defiantly, through the sixty men assembled for morning community meetings, always sitting up front. She appreciated not being bothered by the male vets (this time they stayed away, not certain where she stood on the gender spectrum). But at the same time, she was lonely. "I'm the only one of my kind," she once remarked.

J-Hi and I built a strong therapeutic tie. She had a history of clashes with staff, and was the butt of jokes by those who had previously worked with her. I defended "my girl." I taunted them: "Hey,

aren't we supposed to be an empathic therapeutic community?"
That stopped them.

To me, this veteran was fun. "I have nothing to wear!" she
would say, rolling her eyes in mock exasperation. She gloried in
girlish clothes, and they were very flamboyant—one day, a Scottish
plaid micro mini from a thrift shop called Out of the Closet; the
next, a neon-yellow spandex cat-suit and four-inch strappy stilettoes in which she teetered around managing, somehow, not to fall.
"Looks like a pineapple!" whispered a woman on staff when she
whisked by. J-Hi heard that remark. I could tell, by how forcefully
she whipped her head away, but at heart she was undeterred.

This veteran was through with suffering. She wanted fun, and
she pursued it with a vengeance. She wasn't one to slouch on a bench
smoking cigarettes, waiting for the bus with the guys. She was the
one beside them, grinding her hips and mouthing the words to a
song blasting through headphones. This girl wasn't going to waste
a minute!

And she never took herself too seriously. She laughed in fact,
telling me about the drug-sniffing German Shepherd that stuck its
cold, wet nose up her towel as she stepped out of the shower, still
dancing to a Supremes song. It was 7:00 p.m. and the dogs were part
of a surprise drug raid underway. Said J-Hi, hand clasped over her
heart with melodramatic flair: "What a shock!" Then she sang a few
bars: "Stop! In the name of love!"

Unlike other vets, she was fearlessly honest, at least with me.
She talked about the stepfather who beat her for "acting feminine,"
and how she had been "born with a flick of the wrist." She explained
that in her teens she thought, "I'm just not sexual", and in her twenties "tried" to be heterosexual but "didn't like it." She spoke about
the deep personal isolation she felt at having to hide her sexual orientation while in the Service, long before "Don't ask, don't tell."

Despite all this, she was not embittered. Winsome, yes—"I'll never have the jaw… or the hands and feet [of a woman]," she said. Enraged, yes, when decrying the traumas of life as a "trannie" (her term): "It's all about how you look, your face, your body, who looks better than who!" She said it was worse than competition between heterosexual women, "because of all that testosterone and violence." But embittered, no.

Unfortunately, J-Hi tested positive for cocaine, as she had twice before, and went AWOL one night. No note, no phone call—typical relapse behavior. I missed her, especially that first day, when I revisited her room, wigs still nailed to the wall, glittery, strappy stilettoes and velvet chokers strewn over the floor.

About a year later, I ran into her at OPCC, the Ocean Park Community Center, a hub of homeless services and temporary housing in Santa Monica, near the beach. She seemed happy, with new therapeutic ties and a sense of acceptance. Heading down the hallway with a laundry basket, she cheerfully greeted residents and staff. But a year after that, she telephoned to ask me about returning to the Dom. "I need help," she said. "I need a connection."

When J-Hi came to my office she did not look well. Her hair was matted and tucked beneath a baseball cap. She was hunched inside the folds of an old, faded pea coat. I explained that the Dom had changed, and that all patients now faced a thirty-day restriction to VA grounds. She declined, obviously still on crack and unwilling to stop.

I haven't seen her in years. I hope she's alive, but when high-risk patients stop showing up, I always wonder. In recent years, the VA has made some advancements in caring for transgender veterans. They not only get their own rooms, but are respected members of the gay—or, to be politically correct, non-normative gender—community. J-Hi would have had an easier time.

I am grateful to her for some measure of enlightenment. She showed me, with far more specificity and candor than any academic or clinical course, that gender can often be a state of mind. She had the clothes, the mannerisms, and more joie de vivre in being female than many of us who were born that way.

A Lot to Digest

So much had happened since 2007: Two tragic deaths. A Democratic administration. A changing American culture and social norms. Two protracted wars. A new generation of returnees.

The VA as a whole, and the Domiciliary in particular, lagged behind. With a flood of troops coming home bearing the wars' signature disorders—TBI (traumatic brain injury) and PTSD (post-traumatic stress disorder)—it was no longer enough to "just house" veterans and refer them to other clinics on VA grounds for actual therapy (the Mental Health Clinic, the Addiction Treatment Clinic). We at the Domiciliary had to offer our own, home-based groups and therapies.

And so, the Domiciliary organization was reconceptualized. Each floor had its own interdisciplinary treatment team (social workers, addiction therapists, vocational rehab specialists), serving specific populations requiring treatment for: combat trauma; substance abuse (one of which I led); homelessness; and unemployment. One small program (at most twenty) was for women. Thus, each team leader had to design a full daily schedule of therapeutic groups and activities.

We were even outfitted with a new name: the Domiciliary Residential and Rehabilitation Treatment Program, or DRRTP. It was a mouthful, for sure; but like everything that came down the pipeline from VA offices in Washington, D.C., we were forced to swallow it whole.

Chapter Seven

HOW TO BUILD A TREATMENT PROGRAM FOR TODAY'S RETURNEES

Game's Over

Step one: Banish bingo. Volunteer Services managed the games, which were held in several windowless, conjoined rooms on the basement floor across the hall from my office. These were gala events: Prizes up to five dollars. Heaps of pink, white and chocolate donuts with sprinkles. Sodas. And Jan! A very cute, petite, blonde facilitator with twinkly blue eyes framed by thick turquoise liner, four-inch stilettos and tight pencil skirts with slits. How could we compete with that?

Staff hated bingo. The lead doctor complained that diabetic patients should not be indulging in donuts. Social workers and psychologists couldn't do timely assessments because the vets would bypass our appointments for bingo. Some of us couldn't concentrate, bombarded by patients' yelps of glee and moans of loss with each letter and number called. There were pre-printed passes requiring signatures from case managers to gain entry, but a crisis arose: Bingo slips were being forged. In fact, my own name was misspelled. What could be done?

"It's very political," an administrator explained. "VA Services provides a lot of gifts and entertainment… We don't want to turn them away."

Thus, for two hours a week bingo trumped therapy, assessments, psychology and social work—not counting the half-hour

smoking break that followed the games. Eventually bingo was ter-
minated, probably by an act of Congress.

A Do-It-Yourself Guide to Building a Treatment Program

With no additional staff, innovation was in order. A VA nutritionist
agreed to teach my vets about "healthy living" (what to consume in
place of alcohol and drugs). I started a "peer group." As described in
an online publication of the federal government's National Institutes
of Health: "Peer support can be defined as the process of giving
and receiving nonprofessional, nonclinical assistance from individ-
uals with similar conditions." This is known as "vet-to-vet" therapy;
patients discuss problems in the absence of staff (great idea—no
drain on overburdened team staffers).

I also launched "Reel Recovery," where we showed movies on
therapeutic topics, such as "Flight," starring Denzel Washington as
an alcoholic airline pilot who eventually becomes sober; "The Silver
Linings Playbook," about mental health recovery; even "Reefer
Madness," the classic 1930s propaganda film portraying the grave
dangers of marijuana, although I was called in to explain its educational value—which was easy. "Reefer Madness" showed the
insanity of: (1) America's failed effort to scare people off of drugs;
(2) the government's false portrayal of the deadly effects of marijuana, long before anyone could imagine it being legalized or used
for medical purposes; and (3) the disturbing gender stereotypes of
dark-haired men in dark suits pushing drugs on innocent young,
unsuspecting fair lasses.

I also started "Understanding Anger," a psycho-educational
series on the biological, medical and psychological underpinnings
of anger. This was not anger management, the treatment du jour
(and a famous movie title). It was hard to picture wounded warriors
holding back anger by counting to ten. A select few, maybe, but
ridiculous for guys used to saying things like, "If a guy gets in my

space, I'm gonna punch him or take him out!" (although they often
didn't mean it). Instead, we talked about the interplay of neurons in
the brain as they influence anger, and referenced Hollywood Bad
Boys—and Girls—Mel Gibson, Charlie Sheen and Britney Spears
(before her recovery). This is a way of "normalizing" anger. The message: Everyone feels anger. How you come to grips with it is what
counts.

"Straight Talk," named after the bus tour of the late Senator
John McCain's failed 2000 presidential campaign, was a discussion
group on controversial news stories of particular relevance to vets:
Should we require U.S. presidents to serve in the Armed Forces?
Should felons be allowed to vote? My goals were: (1) to spark veterans' interest in, and sense of connectivity to, the world beyond
the VA; and (2) to restore confidence, and hope, that their voices
mattered, whether or not they could vote.

What a blast! These guys were wildly enthusiastic, and their
views sometimes surprised me because I, too, had bought into the
American media portrayal of vets as gung-ho, flag-waving rednecks.
Gays in the military? No problem; if a man can save my life, who
cares? Should men and women on active duty be allowed to demonstrate against a war? Absolutely not! Even if you oppose the war in
which you serve, military creed—loyalty, honor—must prevail!

Ironically, our fiercest debate swirled around cigarette smoking.
In 2009, the small northern California town of Belmont passed
legislation which prohibited renters from smoking inside their apartments due to the dangers of second-hand smoke. It was the first
California law of its kind, but the court of veterans' opinion struck
it down, with fury:

"They can't do that, can they?"

"That's not fair! I'd fuckin' burn down the building—sorry for
the French, Mrs. Plate!"

"That's my right as a citizen!"

"Too bad for the other people—they don't have to live there!"

Even non-smokers agreed: "Where does the government stop? Next, you won't be able to have a drink in your own place!"

When class ended, they left in a huff... for a smoke break which, I'm sure, was extra-long.

People ask, why do (all) veterans support Trump? They don't. In fact, the veterans I worked with were Republicans, Democrats, anarchists, libertarians, pacifists... and yes, Trump supporters. One elderly, Caucasian man proudly wore a red baseball cap, every day, that said: "Trump: Finally, a man with balls."

Veterans were aware of the public's misperception that they were "love it or leave it" types, and explained it like this: The majority of political conservatives are in the officer corps, not the rank and file. And it's the officers who dare to speak up. At least, that was their view. In reality, according to reports on the 2019 mid-term elections, 55% of all vets voted Republican, 42% Democrat.

My guys (the rank-and-file types) lacked higher degrees, but were nevertheless smart, motivated, opinionated(!) and grateful for the opportunity to learn. Unlike college students, they didn't cheer when class was canceled. They wanted everything of value they could get.

The Trauma of Trauma

In addition, local and national authorities mandated implementation of a core curriculum. For substance abuse, this meant continuing the "Matrix" groups. This is the so-called evidence-based therapy model favored by the federal government for its organized, manualized and diversified therapy, ranging from the Twelve Steps to cognitive behaviorism. I was neither for nor against the teachings of Matrix—anything that helps anyone maintain sobriety is priceless, since the odds of sustained success are so slim no matter what the program or philosophy. And I tried to stay open-minded because you could never predict what would work, for whom, and when.

Max C, for example, seemed doomed to relapse. At forty-eight, he had been an alcoholic for twenty years, a husband for twenty, and his wife's caretaker for five, following her massive stroke. He was a devoted caregiver, but their sex life wasn't much anymore, so he had multiple extramarital affairs. His wife either didn't know or didn't care. Now well into middle age, Max's drinking had escalated and his life had spun out of control. Yet he hated "that cult" of AA and distrusted the slickness of Matrix, with its emphasis on abstinence. He completed the program anyway and returned to his wife.

About a year later, on the phone making arrangements with VA patient transportation services, the voice on the other end of the line said, "Mrs. Plate! This is Max!" He was now a VA staffer, thank you very much. "I go to AA meetings twice a week," he said. Several times thereafter he came to see me, this middle-aged man, spiffily dressed, carefully coiffed, slim and groomed to perfection. Women on staff took notice; who is that, they asked, smiling skeptically when told the truth. Besides AA, Max told me, anti-depressants improved his mood: "They kill my libido, so I don't want to have affairs. It's great!" Like I said, anything that keeps a person sober is good.

Most treatments for combat trauma require specialized training, such as Cognitive Processing Therapy (CPT) and prolonged exposure therapy (PE). These are manualized, short-term behavioral therapies which can be practiced in groups or individual sessions. But for the majority of patients suffering from dual disorders—PTSD and substance abuse—we used a simpler, more user-friendly therapy called "Seeking Safety." This unique protocol teachers "safe coping skills" to modulate emotional highs and lows, and decidedly steers clear of probing the trauma itself. "You don't get over things," I learned to say in sessions of Seeking Safety. "You get through them."

There was one session of Seeking Safety I wasn't sure I myself would survive.

The topic at hand was "compartmentalization," which means, admitting to the pain of the past while limiting its impact on the present. I remember saying something like, "Imagine you have a drawer. Not for socks, or shirts, but for trauma. You open it up, look at it, feel it, then put it back and close the drawer. You know it's there, but you don't wear it every day." The vets were polite and attentive, but it was hardly a great analogy, so I moved the discussion along.

Suddenly, Terry raised his hand. He was a tall, imposing figure, usually quiet: "You know what's in my drawer?" he thundered. "A gun! That's what you have in the drawer when you grow up in Compton!" Boom! It seemed to come out of nowhere. Terry launched into a lengthy rant about "What it's like where I came from... I'm not going to give up that gun... I have to defend myself..." and recited the litany of crimes he was forced to commit just to survive the ghetto.

It was a stunning teaching moment: Here was a group focused on the subject of PTSD, with a man in the throes of a PTSD flashback! But it was frightening to watch. He trembled and seethed with rage. And he was surrounded by mesmerized—probably stunned—patient spectators. I knew better than to talk him down (that would intensify his anger), or to get physically or emotionally close. I also knew better than to run after him when he walked out. I could not leave the group unsupervised—one veteran's trauma can easily trigger another's.

But what *should* I do? I wasn't sure. So I asked the raging vet's roommate to follow him. My hope was he'd come back to say that Terry was pretty okay but needed a break—and that I needn't stop the class to call the police. Instead, a few minutes later he returned only to say, "He just wants to walk." That didn't make me feel much better, but I learned, just as the group ended, that Terry had already returned to his room.

He came to see me, calm, even apologetic for having disrupted group. "Yeah, sometimes I get like that," he said with a smile. Clearly, the trauma was back in the sock drawer, and this veteran was back in control of himself.

Remembrance of Things Past

"You feel embarrassed to see a psychiatrist," explained Edward, a very proud half-Japanese, half-Korean veteran who had served in Iraq. "You're supposed to tough it out." For four years, Edward hid inside his LA apartment eating pizza and watching TV, his family discouraging him from seeking help. On visits, his father would ask sarcastically, "What's your problem?"

Edward's "problem" was actually two-fold: depression and PTSD. His was "complex trauma," the kind that results not from a single event (a car accident, a natural disaster), but from several traumas over a period of time. As stated by the National Center for PTSD, the nation's leading research and educational leader on the subject, complex trauma "continues or repeats for months or years at a time." One source of Edward's trauma was combat in Iraq. "I did some terrible things," he told me, "and I'm afraid they are going to come back to haunt me."

The other was "secondary trauma," related to his father, who had survived a Japanese internment camp in Southern California during World War II. Like children of Holocaust survivors who grow up hearing all too much (in their minds) about Auschwitz, Edward grew up with tales of his father's internment. This heightened his combat-related anxiety. Worse, his father thought combat trauma couldn't compare to the horrors of being in a displaced persons camp. Edward felt slighted, even by his father's $1000 monthly allowance, because, he said, "I wanted guidance, not cash."

Vowing not to repeat the sins of the father, the veteran finally sought treatment when his own son, age four, said, "Daddy, we don't have fun anymore." The little boy wanted to play outside. Dad preferred to vegetate on the couch, in a dark apartment.

Alas, Edward only stayed in treatment a few days, and did not return.

I understood the shame of addiction—whether gambling, alcohol or drugs—but had underestimated the degree to which mental illness can still be considered a character flaw, particularly in non-Western cultures.

I worked with another young Korean named Jay, an inveterate gambler who poured his wife's college tuition money into blackjack and craps. Repeatedly, I urged him to seek emotional and financial support from his parents. "I can't! It's a Korean family!" was his refrain. "They look at me with shame." I learned then that Asian Americans who are problem gamblers—and there are many in the so-called model minority—face unique roadblocks: a cultural reliance on holistic treatments (rather than Western-based practices); the belief that families should keep problems to themselves; and the relative scarcity of Asian-specific treatment programs in the U.S.

After the divorce, Jay returned to treatment for PTSD, not substance abuse. This, he believed, was at the root of his gambling problem. Many young veterans who served in Iraq and Afghanistan resisted the idea of having dual addictions. One was enough.

Process Group: Steven

What I enjoyed most were the "process groups," but they were uniquely hard to do, as they came with no manual or pre-set lesson plan. Instead, the lessons lie in the interactions of the group. As negative patterns of communication and behavior surface spontaneously, group members learn to give and receive feedback so as to move toward problem-solving.

The process group is a well-known therapeutic staple of the twentieth century, but at the VA, with veterans wary of government, it's particularly difficult to gain trust; and without trust, the group fails.

When they worked, these groups made for some precious moments of trust, caring and emotional awakening. I loved the dramatic tension, and felt privileged to hear firsthand the veterans' deeper truths.

Steven Alvarez had been in the Domiciliary six times. He drank a lot, but his drugs of choice were "downers" (benzodiazepines like Valium, Xanax) and heroin. Once a combat Marine in Vietnam, the vet admitted, years later, that he was stuck in the past: "I never really left Vietnam." Steven was well known to the PTSD clinic. He had completed all the classes and therapies, but suffered many relapses on heroin, downers and alcohol. He was a handsome Latino man, very macho, with a stocky build, a thick, black moustache and dark sunglasses he wore almost always, even in groups, which was against the rules. Claiming extreme sensitivity to light, he begged for exemption, so we gave our consent.

One day, surrounded by about twenty peers, Steven spoke about his feelings of overwhelming guilt: "I used to do heroin with my grown son," he explained. At first, he forced a cynical smile, then leaned back in his chair to prepare for an avalanche of group scorn. There was none. So he went on: "My son overdosed on heroin and died." A tear slid below the dark glasses, down his cheek. No, they were *not* doing heroin together the day "my kid" died. That would have been worse! But Steven knew he had set a lousy example for his son, and, as a drug-using buddy, felt culpable in the young man's death.

Steven was a haunted man. The death of his son, like his days in Vietnam, left him in a state of perpetual anxiety and despair. The only relief came from recreational drugs.

What can a group do to mitigate such pain? We listened, told him we cared and gently reminded him that no man can save another from a drug-induced death. Above all, we didn't judge him or call him a lousy father.

Steven left the program shortly afterward and did not return. He called me once, in what sounded like a drunken stupor, to inquire about Domiciliary readmission. After about five minutes he said, with a thick slur, "I love you, baby."

Then he hung up.

Process Group: Jack

Jack M was a hard case. At fifty-three, he was a curmudgeonly, overweight Caucasian guy who didn't want to be at the Dom and was focused on a single goal: to regain his driver's license, which had been suspended due to multiple DUIs. Jack's drug of choice was meth. A truck driver, he had lost his job, so the Department of Motor Vehicles ordered him to rehab in order to regain his license. One day he blurted out in group, with marked defiance, "On March 16, I'm out of here and working!" Normally, a vet addicted to speed is encouraged to consider another line of work; long stretches on the road, alone, are not conducive to sobriety.

Jack was angry when I said this. "That's treatment hooey!" he shot back, shifting his hefty frame in the small chair. "Anyone who thinks 120 days here is going to accomplish anything is full of it! The real test is in the real world. This little treatment room ain't nothing!"

"It's a start," someone shouted.

But Jack, undeterred, continued his rant, asking me, "What's your success rate for vets achieving sobriety?"

I asked, "What's yours?"

He answered, "Not much."

I rested my case.

His was an easy question with a difficult answer. First, you can't quantify success in the field of substance abuse. How do you define it? Lifelong sobriety? Decades of sobriety, interrupted by a brief period of relapse? Program completion? Another problem: How can you achieve an accurate accounting of patients once they leave treatment? We know who goes into programs, and who stays, but what happens to those who leave and don't return? Do they remain sober? Or not?

While I had won the battle with Jack that day, I knew the war would go on. The burly, obstinate truck driver was not one to surrender.

The following week, Jack was first to raise his hand after my customary opening line, "Who has the burning desire to talk?" Jack announced that he didn't like Twelve Step groups. He didn't like "all this treatment." He didn't like that I hadn't shown him individual attention—so I gave him an appointment for 2:00 p.m. the next day, and he calmed down.

The mad truck driver arrived on time. He talked a lot, about how anxious he was to return to work. How the only thing he did well in life was drive a truck. How he still thought he could drink and escape consequences, now knowing what they were and having suffered accordingly. He also said he was always "fine until something disastrous happens." He was open, if not honest with himself.

Jack talked about "the girl" he once loved—how he proposed marriage on the beach, kneeling next to a heart he had made of driftwood, seaweed and shells. Her answer was "yes," but eight months later she kicked him out of the house. He said he did not know why.

Had he imagined the whole affair?

Had he failed to see that she wasn't a good person?

Had he fallen in love with love, rather than this individual?

Not once did he consider that the meth habit might have played a part. Nor did I say so. For the first time, Jack had opened up to me; this was no time for a challenge.

His was a bleak early childhood history. His mother handed him over to his father after giving birth. Ten years later, the father died. He was then handed over to an uncle and aunt, who beat their new charge with a switch and said, on more than one occasion, "We never should have taken you on." The aunt and uncle finally handed him over to foster care, where his foster parents abused him, physically and verbally. At age twelve, a Boy Scout leader molested him…

Was it all true? Could anyone make this up??

This was another Jack—not the defensive, aggressive attack dog from before but a beaten-down teddy bear, soft at the center, in tatters and in need of deep emotional repair. From then on, he was more collegial in group and friendlier to the other vets.

He completed the program, regained his driver's license and returned to work as a truck driver on March 16.

Just as he said he would.

On the road, again.

Process Group: Peter

Peter was a heavyset, fifty-six-year-old alcoholic, in treatment for the first time. He was earnest and affable, well-liked by both patients and staff. He had a blond handlebar moustache, a belly he patted after every meal and a fondness for barely covering it up with Hawaiian print shirts. Unfortunately, one day the police tossed him in Men's Central Jail on an old "failure to appear" warrant. His veteran buddies, who stood by at the nearby 7-11 convenience store as he was seized, pleaded with me to intervene: "Please help us get him out, Mrs. Plate. You know he's a good guy."

Normally, VA social workers don't mess with the law, but Peter—a "good guy," beloved by his fellow vets—warranted an

exception. I spoke to his public defender, then consulted Domiciliary officials, who agreed that, once released, Peter could return for
treatment. A few days later, he was in fact released.

Mr. Good Guy came back to treatment, but he seemed out
of sorts—listless, unshaven, hair hanging unevenly below his ears.
Worse, he stopped coming to groups, and then one night left the
program. I was surprised, but the vets weren't. Turned out Peter had
relapsed a month before his arrest and had been drinking steadily.
They all knew.

Fool! Blindsided and duped, I could blame only myself.
Patients are not friends—I had forgotten that—and as a result, I
had been pushed into vouching for a veteran in flagrant violation of
the rules, who even involved his teammates in a kind of cover-up. I
had thrown myself into advocacy, despite these embarrassing real-
izations: (1) Drug activity happened on my watch; (2) the patients
were masterful manipulators; and (3) the Good Guy who seemed
so sincere was cheating on the government dole. How I wanted to
believe otherwise! How glorious I felt crusading for Peter's rights!

After that, I vowed never again to retrieve a veteran from jail—
even, and perhaps especially, a Good Guy.

I had loved, lost, and learned.

Processing Out: Me

It was the Monday after Thanksgiving weekend, 2014. Protests had
broken out in Ferguson, Missouri, when the governor announced
that a second grand jury would not be called in the case of Michael
Brown, an unarmed African American teenager shot to death by a
white police officer, who was not indicted. It was one of the first in
a spate of racially charged police shootings that swept the country.

No one on staff wanted to work after the holiday. Some were on
planned leave, others called in sick. So that Monday, I was singly in
charge of sixty vets. That was daunting, and potentially dangerous,

but my many previous efforts at lobbying for standby staff had been to no avail. Thus, I made a command decision: to give the vets a half-day off but in the morning to conduct the main therapeutic group of the day: "Managing Your Mood and Thoughts."

This is a cognitive behavioral group, fairly formulaic. Things should have been orderly.

But they weren't. The moment I stepped into the dayroom, I could feel the vets' unrest. They were fired up from watching the Ferguson riots and protests on TV.

Something else was going on, too: Simon.

Military creed says: Leave no man behind. But that's precisely what had happened to Simon W, one of their fellow vets on the team. They were mad. Simon, recently diagnosed with lung cancer, had been transferred to the "cancer team" in building 217 across the quad. There, surrounded by patients in advanced stages of the disease, he had become depressed. The ailing vet missed his friends on the third floor of building 214, but Domiciliary Assistants did their strongarm thing and blocked his path. A rule is a rule, they told him: You must stay on your own floor. No entry allowed.

So he was turned away. This had gone on for days.

"Let's do Simon!" several called out, at the start of class.

What they meant was, let's make Simon's dilemma the focus of the group. And so, the exercise went something like this:

Simon, who I think they had sneaked in, stood up front in the dayroom, by the erasable board. Prodded by the group, he followed CBT (cognitive behavioral therapy) protocol by talking through his problem, which I summarized by writing brief, encapsulated descriptions under three labeled columns on the board:

(1) Upsetting event: "I was denied access to my third-floor friends."

(2) Automatic, distorted thought and emotion (arising from the event): "No one wants me!"

(3) Rational response (balancing feelings and thoughts): "I still have friends who wish they could visit with me on the floor. I'm not alone."

The fourth and final step involves discussion and group problem-solving. Among the chorus of suggestions from the other vets:

"Communicate."

"Write a letter."

"Talk to the boss of the people kicking him out!

"Go downstairs to see the Dom Assistants now and demand an answer!"

That last comment was alarming. "Not the best idea," I warned. "People downstairs might get upset."

But the veterans had whipped themselves into a frenzy and were ready to march. "Let's go straight to the source! This is our chance!" shouted twenty-four-year-old Phil. Immediately, others joined in—mostly young men whose service in Afghanistan or Iraq (or both) had left them restless and eager for another call to arms.

"Let's go!" Phil said again.

With that, the group rose from the dayroom, like lava, hot at the center, spilling onto the stairway and into the elevators heading downstairs. In seconds, they were gone.

"I'm not sending you," I called out as the last guys left the floor. "But I'm not stopping you, either."

Both were true. I could not singlehandedly restrain thirty guys. There was no time to seek help and consult. And of this, I felt sure: To reside on federal government property does not, and should not, require one to sacrifice his First Amendment rights to freedom of assembly and speech. Those are basic human rights, and aren't veterans humans?

A few minutes—or was it seconds?—later, I took the elevator two floors down to check out the scene. When the elevator doors opened, there was an impressive sight: some thirty guys—homeless, addicted to drugs, on virtually every medication known to man— yet standing at attention: chins up, chests out, shoulders back, arms at their sides. Facing them was Audrey (the sex education VA "lifer"), supervisor of the Dom Assistants, who had been called to the scene because her staff claimed to feel "threatened."

I was worried. Ever since Audrey's poorly received presenta- tion to veterans on the subject of sexual harassment (don't look in a woman's eyes, don't look at "my ass" when I leave the room), she had been eyeing me with contempt. She knew I had reported her to the Domiciliary Chief. She resented having been hauled in for a reprimand.

Meanwhile, Gary, a returnee from Afghanistan, led the Audrey- veterans' face-off. He spoke with elegant calm on behalf of Simon and his fellow vets: "We care about our brother Simon, and we want to know why he's being shut out."

Others spoke up in turn: "We want Simon back!"

"Why can't the guy come upstairs for a cup of coffee?"

Surprisingly Audrey, never one to back down, summoned up a smile and apologized—"I forgot to tell my staff about the special cir- cumstances in this veteran's case," she said, promising to set things straight. That explained it: Those Dom Assistants didn't know that Simon was an exception to the rule. He in fact should have been allowed on the third floor of building 214, and by turning him away, they were violating orders.

Crisis resolved.

With that, the men made an about-face and returned to the dayroom upstairs, where we debriefed. All felt that this exercise in communication had been a success. Relieved, we basked in the warm glow of this shared triumph.

"You stood up for us," Edward told me, twenty-eight-years-old and not one to accept seemingly random assertions of authority from Audrey or her staff.

"What happened in the minutes before I followed you guys downstairs?" I asked.

"Nothing," said a few. No one disagreed.

No arguments? Tensions?

"No," they answered, in a resounding, collective voice.

Nevertheless, I had to wonder. Something felt not quite right. The VA was full of land mines. You never knew what might blow up in your face. As the group drew to a close, I felt twinges of remorse and self-doubt—never trust the VA! Never do anything out of the ordinary! Could this scene really, truly, have been so smooth?

Oddly, I started to feel guilty. Of what? "Supposing I had tried to stop you guys from going downstairs?" I asked.

"That would have been worse," asserted Edward, eyes lowered, his voice a near whisper, as if struggling to keep a lid on deep-seated anger at the thought of anyone—including me—issuing commands.

Four days later, on Friday afternoon, Frances L, the Chief of Social Work for all of the West LA VA, rang me up. This could only be bad news. In twelve-and-a-half years, she had never called. "I need to see you, right now!" she commanded. She would not say why. Fearful and obedient, like a dog cowering before a blow, I drove across campus, under the freeway, slid into a parking space and virtually ran to her office on the sixth floor of the medical center.

Frances was known as "Old VA" (less than two years into the Trump Administration, she left). Once a trailblazer for women of color—one of the first African American women to hold a position of high rank—she was now regarded as a faded movie star. For years she had ruled by nit-picking and fear—"No lunch longer than one-half hour!" "No jeans on Fridays!" and, in one memorable instance from which I was gratefully exempt, she informed a group of social workers, "Your positions are being eliminated"—adding with a chuckle just moments later, as several started to cry—"Just kidding!"

This time, the joke was on me. From her sixth-floor perch, Frances, decked out in her customary Hillary-style pants suit topped off with a 1980s suburban mom wig, explained her summons: "I've had several reports of contact from people at the Domiciliary about your behavior, and I am removing you from your place of work."

Reports? About what?

"Misconduct," she said. "You are under investigation." Then she added, "Don't worry... since 'it' might not even be true."

Frances would say no more, but I knew by then that "it" referred to the veterans' Monday morning march—and some Dom Assistants' complaints. What else?

This was bewildering, though. The event had unfolded without incident (or so the veterans said). How could I be in trouble? Hadn't the Domiciliary Chief, only hours earlier that day, checked off the "Outstanding" box on my performance evaluation?

That was then. This was now. In accordance with standard operating procedure, Frances whipped out the following letter and read aloud:

December 5, 2014
Subject: Detail

This is to notify you that you are being detailed to work in the Substance Abuse Program, building 257, pending the results of an investigation into allegations of misconduct by you. This detail is effective immediately.

Your job title, series, grade, step and pay will not change as a result of this detail. Your tour of duty may need to be adjusted to meet the needs of your detail organization and the patients for whom services are provided.

I interrupted her to say, "I can read!"

Only later, at home, would I read on:

While you are on detail, you are to refrain from coming to Buildings 217 and 214 without specific authorization from me. Additionally, you are to refrain from contacting staff or patients from the Domiciliary Medicine Service during this detail without specific authorization from me. You are to report to your detail supervisor, [name], immediately after you receive this notice. If you have any questions about this notice, you can contact [name], Human Resources.

Chief, Social Work Service
West Los Angeles Department of Veteran Affairs

Instead of signing the letter, which she asked for next, I snatched it from her hands and took off.

The exact charge, spelled out weeks later by someone from Human Resources, was "endangering staff safety." Or, as outlined in Audrey's write-up, "It [the morning the men marched] could have been a huge security concern."

Funny. I was alone on the third floor with a bunch of angry veterans. Audrey and staff were on the ground floor, the entrance to 214 wide open, people milling around the lobby, stopping by the soda machine, drifting in and out. And *they* didn't feel safe?

Like a freight train, the VA wheels went into motion. What did they think? That I would lie down on the tracks?

I'd been working since the age of six. Even in Hollywood, no one had treated me with such disrespect—not Rod Serling, not Alfred Hitchcock, not a single one of the legendary figures with whom I once worked, whose fame and artistry might well have inspired such an imperious and abusive style—not even in the sixties, when child actors were still treated like second-class citizens. All of which is to say, I learned early about unfairness in life, but the punishment Frances doled out seemed astonishingly rough.

And what about my own First Amendment rights?

Never mind. There was no time.

Instead, I took my own time, literally—in the form of paid "stress leave." Easily done: "Andrea Plate would be well advised to take three weeks of sick leave due to stress," wrote my general practitioner, who had interned at the VA.

Could I have held myself together at the VA, banished from the Domiciliary, shuttled off to another clinic, in the throes of anger and despair? Probably, but I was afraid to try... afraid of myself, afraid of losing self-control, afraid that every day on the job my mind would be full of reckless fantasies, like storming through the Domiciliary doors, cursing and refusing to leave the premises (surely VA police would have escorted me out!), or walking into the hospital's Chief of Staff at the medical center, spewing venom about the VA's culpability in patient deaths, just to give him a scare. What good would that do?

Instead, I stayed away and determined how to fight back. To my surprise, two lawyers I called refused the case, and the third suggested not wasting my money or his time. Given no evidence of discrimination on the basis of gender or race, I was not in a "protected class."

I fumed, cried, and railed against the system in interminable phone calls with friends on staff who were equally outraged. What about the paraprofessional social sciences tech who caused a fire but got a ridiculously light reprimand? Why wasn't the guy who actually bit his co-worker forced to vacate the building? We knew why, of course: they were veterans! They were minorities, too—Hispanics and African Americans—except for Stuart, the only Caucasian. Unlike me, they were a protected class. And they knew it.

Meanwhile, veteran *patients* were all but forgotten. Come Monday morning, they wanted to know: Where's our program leader? What happened? When we ask around, why won't anyone tell?

This is standard VA protocol: No witness tampering! No pre-trial prejudicial publicity! No muddying the waters of the investigation! It was like Watergate and the Mueller investigation rolled into one.

Stonewalled, the men who had led the fateful march downstairs, figuring I'd been fired, blamed themselves: It's our fault! Because of us, she's gone! We failed to protect this woman. I let my mother down... I let my wife down... Now I let my program leader down. The one woman who's helping us!

Clearly, I wasn't the only one punished.

Return of the Native

A month later, the first week of January 2015, the leave time expired and I returned to work at my new "place of detail," the Opiate Treatment Program in building 257. It was a quiet morning.

Come lunchtime, I ventured over to the Domiciliary to retrieve my belongings. Who knew how long I would be banned? Or if I would be allowed back? And frankly, would I even want to go back to the scene of my purported crime? Probably not.

Was I a criminal? A burglar? That's how it felt, creeping in noiselessly, head down, staring straight ahead in the building where I had toiled for twelve-and-a-half years. Yes, I'd been granted permission to enter the premises, but it still felt like a stealth move.

Just before entering, some veterans caught sight of me. They were across the quad, in front of building 214. I was at the top of the long, wrap-around handicapped ramp leading into building 217. I was just about to push a steel, two-tiered patient cart (usually used by veterans when they first moved in) to load up my possessions— lamps that had brightened my dreary office, a personal printer, heaps of notes and files—then unload them in the car.

Four of them rushed over. Having survived a lonely Christmas season at the Domiciliary, shoved under the governance of a program leader from another team, they wanted to welcome me back.

The first guy, a tall, lanky alcoholic in recovery, dull blond hair bunched under a baseball cap, stopped midway down the sidewalk, just before the handicapped ramp, pulled the cigarette from his mouth and exclaimed, "Am I glad to see you!" Then he drew in an exaggerated, deep breath for dramatic flair.

Across the quad, some faces peeked above the smoking huddles. The guys waved. A handful more broke free and headed my way. Within minutes, I was encircled by seven or eight veterans. They were excited:

"They did you wrong!"

"What happened was bullshit!"

"Where are you working now?"

"Are you okay?"

"Good for you! You're outta the Dom!"

Just then two men driving off campus—Jorge, a sixty-four-year-old Vietnam combat veteran at the wheel—honked to get my attention, smiled and gestured with a thumb's up.

A few offered to help push the overloaded cart, but I responded with alarm: "No! They'll charge me with marshaling the troops again!"

The vets laughed.

It was a hero's welcome. It was thrilling. But it should have come as no surprise. Veterans are loyal. Intensely loyal. They can be nasty and assaultive, entitled and aggressive—but when they have your back, they will not let you fall. No man, or woman, will be left behind.

Most astounding, however, was what happened later that day. I had no idea that, during my paid leave, the veterans had banded together to compose a letter of protest on my behalf. They had presented it to Domiciliary administration—and gotten no response. Still, they held onto the letter.

I learned all this at 3:00 that same day, when Eduardo came to see me at the Opiate Treatment Program up the hill, where I'd been banished while waiting for the investigation to conclude. As "head writer," Eduardo presented me with a laminated copy of the letter. It read:

Subject: Andrea Plate, LCSW

My name is _____, Vietnam Veteran who served in the Marine Corps and a resident of the Domiciliary Building 214, Room 213, Bed 2.

On the morning of December 1, 2014, Mrs. Plate knowing that she was going to facilitate the meeting on "Managing Moods and Thoughts" for the person that does this function and who was not available. Prior to the meeting Mrs. Plate approached me and asked if I would want to assist her with the facilitating

and I responded by letting her know that we have an
upsetting event that has affected the entire veterans
on the floor. I briefed her in on the situation and
I included (patient name) and (patient name), at
no time was Mrs. Plate directly involved in what
transpired after that.

She (Mrs. Plate) stayed back and listened and at times
asked other veterans to offer suggestions, while she also
in turn offered suggestions. She did not instigate any
prohibited action for or against staff; she was merely
there as always for moral support.

Where there is only speculation that she has been
disciplined, please do not let this be true and give us
some assurances that it is indeed speculation. Mrs.
Plate fully supports veterans in their recovery process
and she would never misguide us in any form or
fashion. I have asked other veterans to endorse this
document in support of Mrs. Andrea Plate, LCSW.
By providing their signature and providing their room
and bed number.

I remain respectfully,
[Patient signature]

On the reverse side were the signatures of thirty veterans.

This was one of the most touching moments of my VA career. It was also a great teaching moment for the vets, who obviously felt that their take-charge group effort, in support of a just cause (me), mattered. Although their letter had been ignored by administrators, it melted a certain social worker's heart.

A Moving Target is Harder to Hit

In truth, the infamous "detail" provided much-needed respite—from the staff wars and the enormous strains of residential programming. In fact, I wound up happily "detailed" to the Opiate Treatment Program.

The OTP seemed like a mom-and-pop shop where people got along. Like at all outpatient clinics (compared to a residential program such as the Domiciliary), patients came to groups, then left. They showered, shaved, ate and slept in community programs or their own homes. Most cleared out by 3:00 p.m. It was a lot easier than the Forbidden City of the Domiciliary.

Five months passed. I fully expected to stay at the OTP; but alas, it came as no surprise when I was summoned back to the Domiciliary to meet with the Chief. She presented me with a letter of exoneration, mandating my immediate return to the Domiciliary. "We're glad to have you back!" said the Chief. She gushed. She smiled.

"There's just one problem," I said. "I don't want to come back." Then she feigned shock.

"Would you want to work with people who railroaded you out of here?" I asked. "After this low-tech lynching?"

That poor Chief. A sharecropper's daughter, this remark must have hit her hard. Then she tried to appease me.

First she encouraged me to read my personnel "file on the detail," which I did, courtesy of the Freedom of Information Act. Three paraprofessionals had written notes with statements ranging from: "She sent a mod [sic, mob, of veterans] looking like they were up to no good" to "I was scared." But Audrey's narrative was surprisingly evenhanded, although it concluded that "Andrea Plate sent these veterans" into what "could have been a huge security issue".

Then she encouraged me to choose the position to which I would return. There were three options available. One was to return

as program leader within the Domiciliary (Been there, done that!!).
The other two were to be situated elsewhere, while serving as a liaison between the Domiciliary and other on-campus VA sites.

I am a woman of my word. When banished from the Dom, my thoughts were: Never again! Do not go back! Incompetence and chaos are tolerable. Evil is not.

Remembering this, I accepted a position at "Cal Vet," the California State Veterans Home, situated about a half-mile up the hill from the Dom. A year earlier, the state and federal governments had formed a partnership program headquartered in the state home. The feds needed someone there to represent the VA—in particular, the Domiciliary. The state home was sleek and modern, with well-tended gardens, upscale furnishings and no Domiciliary staff. It sounded ideal.

Chapter Eight

STATE OF SIEGE: THE CALIFORNIA
STATE VETERANS HOME
2015–2016

They called it "Guantanamo Bay," this state-run residential program for veterans on federal VA grounds.

It wasn't the African gowns, turbans and hijabs worn by staff, many of whom were immigrants from around the globe (Korea, Nigeria, Ghana, the Philippines and "one of those Muslim countries"), that troubled the veterans. It was the feeling that staff didn't care about them. By comparison, I was known as the caring Caucasian.

This was my chosen place of work following expulsion, exile and exoneration from charges of misconduct. I was stationed at THP, the Transitional Housing Program—brainchild of the federal government, an arranged marriage of two government bodies (the state and the federal VA) with clashing management styles and political missions. Its purpose, stated publicly, was to serve patients who had finished Domiciliary residential treatment for mental health and substance abuse but were not yet ready to leave the grounds and enter what they called "the real world." Here, they would be case managed while searching for affordable or transitional housing and salting away savings from government checks each month. Some even landed jobs and saved income.

This newly constructed Cal Vet in LA was actually the eighth state home. The seven built before, once called "old soldiers' homes," had been serving the elderly and disabled since the Civil War.

But the THP, where I worked, was entirely new. It comprised eighty beds, all filled by Domiciliary "graduates," housed on the ground floor. The three floors above were reserved for permanent housing, filled by disabled veterans paying rent.

There was a political pay-off to this arrangement. The Cal Vet street address, 11500 Nimitz Avenue, on VA grounds, registered in some important national database as "permanent housing." Thus, the eighty men in my charge, on the ground floor at that same address, were counted as "successfully housed"—when in fact they were homeless, and in many cases without jobs and incomes. This was a short-cut and a sham. Nevertheless, announcements about markedly improved housing statistics were applauded and cheered around the VA. It was like false body counts of Vietnamese reported by the 1960s–70s media, to make it look as though Americans were winning the war.

Keystone Cops

I got an urgent phone called from a social worker at the Addiction Treatment Clinic (ATC), situated in building 258, across the parking lot from Cal Vet.

"He's very intoxicated in his room!"

She was referring to Adolfo, who had been attending her alumni sobriety maintenance group at the ATC but had suddenly stopped showing up. The patient's room was at the end of a long, carpeted Cal Vet hall. Adolfo was a friendly sixty-eight-year-old widower with a grandfatherly look—white beard, white Afro—suffering from severe alcoholism and depressive disorder.

"Come in!" he said, after I ran and pounded on the door.

Adolfo lay in bed, in striped pajamas, his head propped up on pillows. Usually reserved if not withdrawn, he greeted me with a loopy smile.

"You're drunk," I said.

"Yup!" He laughed and pointed to an empty, giant-sized bottle of scotch on the counter nearby.

First, I left to fetch other staff. It's a bad idea to be alone in a room with a drunk veteran, however friendly.

I returned with two people: the social worker employed by the state—"Joseph," a South Korean new to LA who used that name because he was tired of people tripping over his Asian name; and "Eddy," the Nigerian-born head honcho on the floor, also employed by the state, also compelled to adopt a user-friendly name.

The patient was drunk, but he spoke the truth.

"I lasted sixty days," he said, laughing again and pointing to a brown paper bag containing three additional bottles of scotch—one empty and two full, although all three were smaller than the one he had consumed in private.

This was a tough situation. At my old place of work, the Domiciliary, I would have known just what to do:

(1) Find someone to escort the inebriated patient to the ER for a medical evaluation, which would result in either clearance to return to the program or hospital admission for medical detox; and

(2) Get a psychiatric evaluation, because the population at highest risk for suicide is elderly, Caucasian men who live alone, with additional risk factors including a history of suicidal ideation (thinking about suicide) and/or past attempts. Fuzzy-haired, elderly Adolfo met all the demographic and historical criteria for suicidality, except race (he was African American, not Caucasian).

But I was in a new job, and I was up against the state. The state-side social worker, Joseph from Korea, was smart. Given the thickness of his accent, though, he considered it best not to talk. But social workers are supposed to be communicators! By contrast, Eddy from Nigeria spoke the Queen's English but had no clinical sense. He had previously served as a security guard.

Eddy took charge that morning, first by donning plastic gloves to seize the alcohol, then by spewing a series of questions to the patient:

"Have you eaten?"

"Not for a day."

"Would you be willing to eat?"

"Sure."

And, most improbably, "Are you going to be okay in this room tonight?"

"Oh sure, sure."

"He's having a blast!" I interjected. "More fun than we are!"

The old man in striped pajamas smiled and nodded in agreement.

"You'll stay in your room overnight?" Eddy asked.

"Oh, yes, yes." (And why not? Easy!)

Eddy from Nigeria said he would order cafeteria staff to bring dinner and breakfast to the veteran in his room. "I don't want the others to see you," he explained. And that's how this elderly, high-risk patient was left, overnight.

And yet, I did not speak up. You'd think the victories, the right choices, the moral imperatives of a social work career would stick with you forever. But they don't. Sometimes you slip up. Tired, depleted and sick of arguing with staff, I let the matter go, and went home to prepare for the next day's battles.

Fortunately, Adolfo followed orders and was fine the following morning. He had stayed in his room, eaten dinner and kept clear of his scotch. And, to my surprise, he agreed to resume attending the Addiction Treatment Clinic just across the way—not because he wanted to be sober, he assured me, but because "I don't want to get kicked out." As far as I know, he stayed sober until his discharge months later, to the Cal Vet state home in Barstow.

After that, I lost track of him.

Losing track

It happens, and for a long time, you may not notice. You forget about former patients. They leave the premises and they leave your mind. This is an inevitable casualty of working with veterans. Each man on your caseload has myriad problems: medical, mental health, substance abuse, legal, housing... or any combination thereof.

The saddest times, for me, were when former "MIA" patients (Missing in Action from the VA campus) finally turned up—dead. Sometimes, for no apparent reason, a particular name and face would come to mind. Then I'd asked around: "Have you heard from so-and-so?" Or, "Anything new with that guy, remember, what's-his-name, the one who..."

A favorite of mine was William, a Vietnam combat veteran, half-Cherokee, also an inspired jewelry maker and lifelong heroin addict. At our last meeting, he greeted me warmly. Happy and relieved to see him, I shook his hand—firmly. William flinched in pain. That hand had become abscessed from shooting heroin into its veins. A nurse from the Opiate Treatment Program, where William had been receiving methadone maintenance treatment, told me he had relapsed and died. That's all she knew. We agreed that it's hard to keep track.

Turf Wars

If the Dom was known as "Club Fed," Cal Vet was called "the Ritz." It had: carpeted floors; long, curved corridors walled in by glass; immaculate gardens; sitting rooms with free coffee and crushed ice; flat-screen TVs; and two cafeterias (one for the general population, one for "my guys" in transitional housing). My friends at the Dom were envious—there were no rats trapped between the walls and under the ceiling tiles as there had been in my previous office; the windows had been cleaned at least once since the Vietnam War; and there were private staff bathrooms rather than those at the Dom (denounced as "elitist" because you had to have a key to get in—no veterans allowed).

The possibilities seemed endless! Finally, a chance to exercise independent judgment, take unilateral action and forge strong inter-governmental ties.

Or so I thought.

These plans were predicated, alas, on two wrong assumptions: (1) that federal government trumps state government; and (2) that the state is subservient to the feds. Not so! I waited a month for clearance of state-approved fingerprints—despite twelve years of clearance at the federal-level VA. During that time, I was permitted to "visit" Cal Vet but forbidden to officially "work" on the premises. So I actually spent all day in the state home, talking to veterans and handwriting notes, before trekking downhill to the Domiciliary, to input those notes in a federal VA computer.

It was crazy. Both governments had their own computer systems, so state staff could not access VA records, and I, a federal employee, could not access those of the state. But we shared patients! Thus, our joint meetings, which were supposed to be bilateral talks, lacked all the essentials of communication, such as shared information and an interpreter. A month later, once settled at Cal Vet, I had a VA computer, a state office with a state phone, and a printer from home that both state and federal support techs refused to hook up for "legal reasons." Even a car crash once devolved into a turf war; both drivers were residents of Cal Vet, but they had collided on a VA, federal government road. Which police jurisdiction should be involved?

There were class wars, too. State staff looked askance at its ground floor residents as "those people," and "the homeless types." They preferred paying customers with supportive wives to push wheelchairs and donate funds. They liked the very old, disabled men neatly tucked into beds upstairs, compliant with (or at least unable to resist) the ministrations of skilled nursing, assisted living and long-term care. The lower caste, on the lowest floor, tried to laugh it off: "We're no-good junkies," they would say, while some even felt compelled to counsel me: "Don't feel bad, Mrs. Plate. We're used to it."

I did not take this well, I admit. When Christmas came, the floors above were lavishly decorated with tinsel and wreaths, while I had to lobby for a single tree to deck the halls below—not what I was trained for in social work school, but it was a fun fight for a good cause, and the tree, although a bit small, added much-needed cheer. It was just a little bit like Christmas.

Check Points

Daily room checks are a staple of residential programs. They enhance patient safety; establish codes of cleanliness and conduct; and encourage patient accountability. Nevertheless, Cal Vet staff did not, and would not, conduct them. "I don't want keys," Eddy the Nigerian honcho told me. "It's too much responsibility."

This meant that, except for security guards manning the building, no one had emergency access to the rooms.

How strange! I was used to Domiciliary policy, which called for daily room checks, nightly bed counts and monthly hall/room inspections. In my twelve-and-a-half years there we seized many varieties of forbidden goods and contraband, including snacks past their expiration dates, alcohol bottles (empty and full), and golf clubs that could be—and had been—used as weapons in roommate fights. In truth, it was fun cruising through the halls and rooms, in this locker room atmosphere of Laker Girl calendars, framed photos of long-lost children and wives, and, in one memorable instance, a package of neon-colored condoms (the patient told me. "They glow in the dark!").

Obviously, a program that houses high-risk patients requires rules. Alas, Cal Vet had few. Patients could come and go at will—with no limits as to where, how far or for how long. One day Ricky, a sixtyish Vietnam combat veteran, stopped at my doorway to say goodbye. He was going to "hang" in the "beautiful Philippines with my girl," he said. Really? While enrolled in a U.S. government program?? Hold his bed for a month? What could I say but, "Enjoy yourself"? Surely, he would. (Of note, several veterans had wives or girlfriends in the Philippines. "She's an old-fashioned girl," they would say, or "She wants to come with me, to the U.S.")

Truth is, due to the excessively hang-loose atmosphere of this unique program, from the moment it opened horror stories had abounded—for example, that a resident lay dead in his bed for thirty-six hours before anyone knew.

It was true.

No public explanation was given, but when I transferred there, and learned that there were no daily room inspections as well as easy staff access, I understood how it could have happened. I learned more about this particular case from Robert H, a patient and former roommate of the deceased, who recounted the dying man's words: "Stay away from me and leave me alone!" Robert, a rail-thin, malnourished-looking, severe alcoholic suffering from cognitive decline, took those words literally and did not look his roommate's way. At all.

You're not dead until someone notices.

State Warfare

Before long, I felt proud to be part of the VA. The State of California staff had virtually no knowledge of the delicate interplay between patient care and national politics. They had business sense (I suppose) but no clinical training, so I was often able to outmaneuver them or win arguments by tossing words and phrases—"psychosis," "cognitive decline"—right over their heads, to induce fear. Sometimes, though, we battled: me against them, the VA versus the state, woman (one) versus men (at least two). Occasionally, they dismissed my concerns as "a VA thing."

The first week, we clashed over John T—a beer-bellied Vietnam veteran with chalk-white skin, dyed ebony hair, a barrel chest and a marvelously cartoonish macho strut. He was also a war hero with several Bronze Stars (awarded for heroism or meritorious conduct in combat). Honorably discharged from the Army four decades ago, he had been battling alcoholism and PTSD since his return from Vietnam.

The crisis arose when Cindy, a front office clerical worker, accused the patient of sexual harassment. Cindy was likeable, but hardly a pillar of stability. An avowedly stressed single mother, she frequently cried or, alternatively, giggled and gossiped so closely with the resident vets that they thought she was their friend.

One day, most unexpectedly, Cindy carried a colorful bouquet with an attached note—"Love you to the moon, and back. John"— to the executive floor. There sat Jason, head honcho of the whole Cal Vet state home—all four floors. His response was to call an emergency meeting mandating the patient's discharge. Make no mistake, this honcho wasn't concerned about the staffer or the patient. An appointee of Governor Jerry Brown, he was concerned about the bigger and better state job he saw ahead, and was determined not to mess up. The words "sexual harassment" seemed to scare him.

Head Honcho Jason, whom I nicknamed Little Caesar, was a very short guy—in my three-inch heels, we stood eye-to-eye—but he had a huge Napoleon complex that inspired him to cut people down to (his) size. Staff spoke of him in hushed tones, and in his presence, they scurried for cover. I, however, was spared all that. An employee of the federal government, stateside Little Caesar held no power over me, so I could walk tall, even at five feet.

It was 2014, just a few years before sexual misconduct charges became everyday news. I would not make a federal case out of John's bouquet. I felt compelled to protect the VA, my job and, of course, John. But Little Caesar expected me to take him at his hallowed state word, telling me, "We've already looked into this" and that there had been "other incidents" between staffer Cindy and patient John. I had two objections:

(1) State staff, by its own admission, had kept no notes or records of previous "incidents." So, I toed the VA line: If it's not documented, it didn't happen (remember the Chart Room and my over-the-top leap?).

(2) The man in my charge deserved a decent defense; so I asked why, if there were previous offensive and inappropriate gifts, Cindy had accepted them all?

Little Caesar would not be budged. He didn't seem to care that John was a decorated Vietnam combat veteran, a longtime frequenter of the VA and someone who, over the years, had cultivated close political connections at several levels of government.

"If you discharge him," I warned, "he will go to his Congressman."

Little Caesar dismissed me with a wave of the hand. "We can handle it!" he said, but I knew he was bluffing. All of our heads were caught in the Obama administration policy vise: You cannot put a veteran on the street—whatever the circumstances.

Game on. Chaos was set in motion. I called John to say I had been ordered to give him an "administrative discharge" (meaning, by orders of the state, not the VA). He was in downtown LA when

I called, getting his Cadillac serviced. Again. It was a 1950s model, gold and white, and he loved it. "I'm a Bronze Star veteran!" he bellowed into the phone. "When I'm done here, I'm going straight to my Congressman." I relayed these words to Joseph, the state social worker, who hurried upstairs to tell Little Caesar.

The following morning, Eddy from Nigeria, who had no problem leaving an intoxicated, elderly patient alone in his room overnight—asked me, "What is your next intervention with John?"

Turned out, Little Caesar had gotten cold feet and canceled John's discharge. Just as I predicted!

Nevertheless, I feigned confusion: Didn't he and Little Caesar have the patient's discharge under control? After all, hadn't *they* insisted on John's discharge, despite my warning that he would appeal to his Congressman? Yes, I had relayed the bad news to the patient, but clearly, I was the messenger of a decision made by state staff.

Instead, I decided to kill him with kindness, ever so politely refusing further involvement in the case on the grounds that it would be "highly ineffectual" because: (1) the patient had called their bluff; (2) by buckling under the veteran's threat and reversing command (instead of listening to my words of caution), state authorities had forfeited credibility; and (3) a vase of flowers does not make a case for sexual harassment.

Eventually, John was sent back to the Dom. The arrangement was far from ideal, he admitted, but it was free, and better than "Guantanamo Bay," his favored moniker for Cal Vet. As a token of appreciation, the Bronze Star veteran gave me a bouquet of flowers before he left—they were paper-made—and there was no attached note, so I thanked him and put them on display in the nearby sitting room. But when I left the VA, I took them home. It was a modest cluster of orange, white and purple paper blossoms in a small glass vase, but to me, it signified much more: That a Bronze

Star veteran struggles long after he leaves Vietnam. That a war hero can be treated as an enemy of the state. And that to keep such a man off the streets is safer, kinder, and better for all.

Several months later, John disappeared from the Dom, and his gold-and-white Cadillac was towed away.

Muster the Troops

When a man dies and it takes one-and-a-half days to notice, something is wrong.

Cal Vet created "muster sheets" ("muster," as defined by the dictionary, is "a formal gathering of troops"). These were 365 pieces of paper, one for each day of the year, bound in a large spiral notebook which the residents were required to sign.

In this way, state staff hoped to keep better track of its residents, whether dead or alive. What they failed to foresee was:

(1) No one on staff was held responsible for checking the sheets and signatures.

(2) There were no consequences for residents who failed to sign. They weren't kicked out, or disciplined. There was no handwriting expert to verify the signatures—if veterans forged signatures to get into Domiciliary bingo, why not do so at Cal Vet?

(3) Since an ill or intoxicated veteran could probably manage to scribble his name, these muster sheets would do nothing to avert patient crises or deaths. Several times, as I frenziedly searched for a resident rumored to be drunk or on the verge of violent action or, in one case, having thrown a plate against a wall, Eddy from Nigeria and Joseph from Korea asked: "Did he sign the muster sheet?"

That was a big help.

State staff had no idea what it means to "enable" a patient—meaning, in recovery-speak, failing to put forth punitive measures for those who are noncompliant. Case in point: Sally, a high-risk resident—fifty-eight-years old, single and suffering from severe bipolar disorder but unwilling to take psychiatric medications. She frequently failed to sign the muster sheets.

My position was, if Sally couldn't get herself together to sign her name once a day, she shouldn't be allowed to live there. Wasn't that the whole point of the muster sheets? Instead, staff members would go to her room, binder in hand, to request her signature.

Sally was a textbook case of "disorganized behavior," defined in medical terms as someone who demonstrates "a decline in overall daily functioning" and "unpredictable or inappropriate emotional responses." One day, she would stride briskly down the halls wearing crisp white linens, her salt-and-pepper pageboy coif perfectly combed; the next day, she would sleep until noon, buried beneath piles of papers and crumpled clothes on the bed. I was not her case manager. Sally, an African American woman, assumed that she could not—and insisted that she would not—be managed by me, a suspect Caucasian. She demanded a particular African American female social worker who worked conveniently off-site and rarely came around. Still, I felt compelled occasionally, at the very least, to check in on her.

Sometimes, Sally let me into her room, but always quickly ushered me out, with the assurance that she was fine. One morning, I noted that Sally hadn't been seen or heard from in nine days, but Eddy and Joseph—more like, Rosencrantz and Guildenstern—were unfazed. "She could come back to haunt us," I warned them. No, I don't pretend to be prophetic, but I do have clinical sense. It was 2014. Then in my thirteenth year at the VA, I had a good nose for sniffing out impending disaster.

That night, Sally was hospitalized. She hadn't eaten in nine days and could barely hold down water. When I visited her at the hospital days later, she remarked that I was the only Cal Vet staffer who had come to see her. This was bad form! In any decent program, at least one person is assigned to demonstrate good will by making a personal hospital appearance. Sad! She was alone, very sick and clueless as to what she suffered from. Sally clasped my hands and said, "Thank you for coming. They told me I could have died." A short time later, she was diagnosed with heart disease and, once stabilized, discharged to the VA nursing home for more acute care.

Similarly, Steven A had been isolating himself in his room at Cal Vet for four days. Somehow, the three hot cafeteria meals, crushed ice and widescreen TV weren't enough to lure him out. Then at 1:28 a.m., after four days of isolation, while in an alcoholic stupor, he rang the bedside emergency buzzer. According to the next morning's report, overnight staff broke into his room. "I'm drunk and I'm dying," he said. Workers called 911. Steven underwent four days of detox treatment at the hospital. But he was denied re-entry to Cal Vet on grounds of mental health instability.

The system discharged this patient "back home" to Las Vegas, where his brother lived, as well as the girlfriend who had recently left him, which was what had initially ignited these desperate behaviors. Clearing out his vacated room, we found four bottles of Ketel One vodka, one bottle of Absolut vodka, plus a container of bleach—the latter to be ingested in a suicide attempt. Fortunately, the vet chose instead to call night staff for help. Soon the other veterans took to saying, "Don't go to the hospital. Cal Vet won't let you come back."

Who would want to go back there? Anyone with nowhere else to go.

The Fun Times

Life at Cal Vet wasn't all tragedy. At times, it was tragicomic.

Pets were not allowed, but Ralph, who had served in Iraq, insisted that his tiny terrier was a certified therapy dog who deserved admission. (Did they check for certification? No.) When dog droppings were discovered on his roommate's bed, Ralph denied that they were the work of his terrier. Eddy from Nigeria was on the case. He stood in the doorway to Ralph's room, arguing.

"Dog? What dog!" shouted Ralph in the doorway. "I don't have a dog! I don't have a fucking dog!!"

Just then, a canvas workout bag mysteriously crept across the floor. Ralph apologized, unzipped the bag, pulled out the terrier and took it to his girlfriend's house.

Yes, Cal Vet was good for comic relief. As in any residential program, there were roommate fights.

One guy was disgusted to find his roommate engaging in oral sex with his girlfriend. I had to mediate with the directive: No intimate transgressions in the room.

Another vet argued with his roommate for leaving their room a mess, then complained after the roommate apologized and mopped the bathroom floor... with Brut cologne. The Brut gave the complainant headaches!

Two elderly gentlemen fought so forcefully that they hit one another with their walkers (fortunately, no one was hurt).

Maybe the sweetest, most fun times were when the oldest veteran in the entire building, a former opera star well into his nineties and permanently housed upstairs, was wheeled outside to the patio. There, he sang arias in the afternoon sun. Then his caseworkers wheeled him back to the third floor Memory Unit, for permanent residents who suffered from dementia.

Thelma and Louise

It was a blast, driving to beautiful downtown Barstow. A native of LA, I'd never been to Barstow. So what? Not much happens there, but this trip was a must. The recreation therapist and I had learned of an impending sweetheart deal between the Cal Vet state home—the one in West LA, where we both worked—and the one in Barstow, which neither of us had seen. No one on the state staff told us about the plan—not Little Caesar, not Eddy from Nigeria and not Joseph from Korea, who were in on the deal. No one had bothered to inform the veterans, either. And no wonder: Their goal was to rid their lovely West LA facility of the homeless, poor and disabled veterans on the ground floor. Then it could be opened to paying customers. By shipping the vets off to Barstow, they could: (1) make a profit; (2) get rid of the freeloaders; and (3) avoid being charged with rendering them homeless.

Barstow, a small desert city located halfway between LA and Las Vegas, is a far less desirable locale than the posh Brentwood district of West LA. This meant that the Barstow home had "more space" to accommodate—make that, dump—the guys in transitional housing. In addition, surely Little Caesar craved the plaudits he'd get for moving non-paying drug abusers off the premises. He gave no consideration to clinical matters. How do you pull a man away from what little social support he may have in LA? Without asking him? Or his social worker? What about disrupting someone mid-course in therapeutic treatment for, say, PTSD?

This state of affairs motivated Keri, the recreation therapist—a young, rebellious state employee who really cared about the veterans—to hijack a state van (the trip was not officially approved) and ask me to go along as the "VA person." Of course! Why not? I wasn't about to let the state staffers pull a fast one on us.

We were good guides. Keri provided Subway sandwiches and sodas (no state food or snacks for unofficial trips), and drove the van down Interstate 15 to Barstow. Meanwhile I, in the passenger seat, joked and did ad hoc therapy with the five guys in back. It should have been a 1.5-hour drive, but it actually took about two hours, given all the "smoke [cigarette] stops." But the closer we got to Barstow, the deeper the veterans' concerns: "Where is this place, the end of the world?" they asked. We drove on through the Mojave Desert, stopping for more smoke breaks (the single non-smoker enjoyed himself by videotaping tumbleweed).

At long last, we reached a hilly road named Veterans Parkway, marked by a sign with an arrow pointing upward. Keri drove up the long, steep hill—maybe a mile. How could this Barstow home be wheelchair-accessible? Aren't a good number of our vets disabled? But even an athletic veteran would need a car to get up or down the hill. None of the visiting vets owned cars. As residents, then, they would live in total isolation in a home on a hill, in the Mojave Desert. Upon reaching the top, they had already written the place off: "There's nothing here! Forget it!"

Nevertheless, we traipsed through the tour, two staffers and five vets, pretending to be fascinated by the small, sparsely furnished rooms; the grounds, including a magnificent view overlooking Barstow; and the recreation rooms (nothing doing that day, although the events calendars showed a lot of scribbling).

Fortunately, the sweetheart deal turned sour due to bickering between the West LA VA state home and the Barstow home. In the end, just three men from my workplace in West LA were transferred there: Denny, a diabetic double amputee in a wheelchair bent on consuming sugar until his death (who didn't even come with us that day); Robert H, the emaciated, recovering alcoholic with cognitive deficits who once roomed thirty-six hours with a corpse, without knowing it; and the elderly Adolfo, once drunk in his room but now sober, who admitted that he looked forward to leaving Cal Vet and grabbing a drink.

Makeshift Marriott

Back home in West LA, the ambience of the Cal Vet state home was consistently and annoyingly upbeat. Twice weekly a chirpy female voice broadcast over the PA system: "The barber's in the house! Hurry on up!" She was particularly perky around Christmastime: "Let's trim that hair below the ears for the holidays!"

Once per month, a different female voice announced power shutdowns designed to check out the emergency back-up system. She spoke in breathy, almost orgasmic tones: "Are you ready? Thirty minutes! Here it comes!" Then the building went dark, the doors didn't slide, the elevators stopped and business ground to a halt. At these times I napped, texted or, on rare occasions, met with veterans in the dark; as a VA employee, albeit in a state-run building, I was exempt from the practice drills.

State staff seemed to have more respect for safety rituals than for homeless veterans. I remember one memorable fire drill, when the designated site of the pretend fire was the storage room next to my office. Eight staffers converged on the scene—some breathless from running with large canisters, all of whom stopped at the "fire scene," nozzles mid-air, aimed at the door… but the pretend fire site was locked. "Who has the key to the storage room?" someone asked. No one. Not even the security guards. Just Francisco, a floor manager who was on leave that day. Embarrassed, nozzles down, they retreated to the safety of their work stations.

Drug-Free versus the Freedom to Use Drugs

Drugs and alcohol were everywhere at Cal Vet, just as they were everywhere on the VA campus. No one is restricted from entering these federal government grounds. Unless someone calls the police, drug business as usual goes on.

There was one big difference, though, with the state-run Cal Vet: Drugs and alcohol were freely and openly abused on the premises after hours, or so I was told. How could this be? One, I was the sole steady VA presence on the floor—among eighty veterans. Two, state staff had no moral or professional interest in these needy veterans, so it was a hang-loose kind of place where everyone but me preferred to look the other way. Three, night watch security guards, the only staff present after hours, didn't care who used and, in some cases, gave the residents a free pass just to be nice. And four, since there were no daily room checks, there were ample opportunities to stash drugs and alcohol in the rooms.

Many mornings, veterans who actually cared about staying clean would greet me to say, "So-and-so had to hold onto the railing to get to his room last night," or, "The minute you guys leave, she comes into the lobby with a glass of wine" (a reference to poor Sally, the bipolar, non-medicated patient who wound up in the hospital).

With no on-site addiction therapist, no urinalysis tests or breathalyzers, and no sobriety groups other than a twice-weekly Twelve Step meeting (attendance was optional), how could anyone expect otherwise?

I believed all of these negative reports. But what could I do? Accuse people of being high on the basis of hearsay? Advocate for drug and alcohol tests? I'd already tried, to no avail. Gov. Jerry Brown's state appointee never listened; neither did Obama's people. No one representing the state had clinical responsibilities. They didn't need, or want, all the fuss of interventions and therapies! The care afforded our returning veterans is only as good and caring as staff at the clinical level can make it—often in defiance of directions from above.

Law and Order

With no one to lean on, I forged ahead. My plan was to become the social worker of law and order. Therein I established the following Cal Vet rules:

(1) All veterans with a documented history of substance
    abuse must attend once-weekly recovery meetings
    in building 257, the outpatient Addiction Treatment
    Clinic (ATC) just across the parking lot.
(2) All patients who relapsed while residing at Cal Vet—
    like the elderly Adolfo, found drunk, in bed—were
    mandated to attend sobriety groups three times
    weekly.
(3) Anyone who refused to attend and suffered a second
    relapse would be transferred back to the Domiciliary
    to restart treatment.

"It's gotten a lot better," the residents told me, referring to the
fact that, with those rules in place, there was less drug abuse and it
was less brazen. But as the sole on-site enforcer, I could not prevail
more than a few months.

Nor was every veteran on my side, particularly those who
preferred to stay high. "I've already done the sobriety thing," they
would say. For months I stood my ground, but it inevitably gave way
beneath my feet. The higher-ups, state and federal, were no help.

Perry H, a veteran of the Iraq War, suffered from schizophrenia
and marijuana addiction. For years, I had mistakenly believed that
marijuana was not harmful. But the marijuana I was thinking of
dated back to the sixties. Today's is much more potent. It surprised
me, at first, to see veterans crippled by dependency and even hallucinating on the drug. To complicate matters, Perry smoked inside
his Cal Vet room. But state workers weren't concerned. "At least it's
marijuana, not cocaine," said a fatigued Joseph from Korea. My
argument was that fire doesn't discriminate between drugs, and
that smoking marijuana on federal government property is prohibited by law (this was before legalization), even if prescribed by an
outside MD. (If caught, who would be blamed? The social worker

who knew and didn't tell.) Another concern was the unmistakable smell of marijuana wafting down the halls. For some, weed was the "gateway drug" that could lead to more serious types of substance abuse.

I worried about Perry, so stoned and psychotic that he couldn't possibly take care of the kids he referenced daily in his psychotic ramblings. I gathered that they were in foster care, but Perry's drug-fried, scrambled brain rendered it impossible to communicate clearly. Sometimes I corralled Eddy from Nigeria or Joseph from Korea to Perry's room, where he was usually locked in the bathroom, refusing to come out. "What do you guys want from me?" he would shout. "I'm on the toilet!" The one time he did emerge, wearing sweatpants but no shirt, he glared at me with wild, marijuana-glazed eyes and screamed, "How dare you come into my room when I'm naked!" I sped off.

Finally, within a month, Eddy caught Perry holding a joint and a Ziploc baggie filled with pot. This sealed the deal for discharge. Knowing this, Perry disappeared that night, only to return a few weeks later to the Domiciliary, for treatment and residential care.

For the homeless veterans on my watch, there was virtually no mental health or medical oversight. The state home employed just one other person from the VA, full-time—an MD, but she presided over the entire facility from her perch on the executive floor. When the eighty vets of the federal/state THP program moved in, she realized she couldn't possibly oversee their care without additional funding and staff. Her only choice, then, was to refer my guys to clinics elsewhere on VA grounds, known as HPACT (Homeless Primary Care Treatment)—about a mile away, on the south side. How unjust! The HPACT clinics served homeless walk-in veterans who had no steady clinic affiliation. Now the Cal Vet guys, who had been on campus up to two years, graduated from the Domiciliary program and remained in good standing at the Cal

Vet home, were thrown into that mix. For some, it was easier to let their health go.

Endgame

There was no coordinated care. What happened to Sally, the patient who hid behind her closed bedroom door for nine days and ended up almost dying at the medical center, shouldn't have happened, of course. Actually, she was affiliated with the Women's Clinic (in the main hospital), but no one situated at Cal Vet monitored her record of attendance or adherence to pharmaceutical or psychiatric regimens. You have to be close by, on site, to keep careful watch. Similarly, no medical staffer monitored a veteran named Jimmy, a diabetic with uncontrolled blood sugar levels who resisted medical care because he thought he could "take care of myself."

Several times, Jimmy collapsed into unconsciousness. Once, paramedics came but promptly left when Jimmy regained consciousness, because he refused transport to the ER about a mile away. Forcing him into the ER van would have violated both VA policy and the law. The second time Jimmy dipped into a coma, he failed to immediately snap out of it. He was hospitalized, then released but prohibited from returning to Cal Vet due to his history of medical instability and noncompliance. A while later I heard that the veteran went back East to be with his long-lost father, then a few months later I heard that he died.

Peter K refused to take medications, and no one on-site at Cal Vet monitored his care. He was a tall, husky, baby-faced returnee from Iraq, age twenty-seven, with icy-blue eyes that cast an eerie, wild stare. For weeks, Peter's behavior had been erratic—hiding in his room as though it were a bunker, darting to and from the building in bouts of paranoia, disappearing late at night until finally, one night, he failed to return. The next week I spotted him asleep in his car. The veterans explained: Peter had recently come into an inheritance. On an extended, psychotic spending spree, he gave $2000 in cash to a fellow vet in need of a car. Now, Peter was penniless.

Then there was Tim, a pudgy, pumpkin-faced middle-aged man with a history of depression and a deep addiction to depressants (Vicodin, OxyContin, Valium, Librium). He had a big heart, he was a good listener, and, as one of the first residents at Cal Vet, he was something of a guru to his fellow residents. But after two years on VA grounds, Tim was ready to move on and "go home." He explained that family in Santa Rosa was willing to give him another chance. "I'm lucky," he told me the Friday morning before leaving on a weekend pass. "For a long time, my mom didn't trust me, but I think now I've gotten her back."

Monday morning, Tim's mother, father and brother appeared at Cal Vet. They said they were there to "pick up his things." As it turned out, Tim didn't make it to Santa Rosa. Instead, he checked into a Quality Inn and died. He had planned on "partying," ordering room service and wearing "one of those hotel bathrobes," said his fellow vets. He had invited these same guys to the motel, but "it didn't seem like a good idea," said little Joey, one of his best friends. In fact, nobody went.

Tim died of an overdose of opiates and probably benzodiazepines. The pills that killed him had been prescribed, yes—by separate clinics, none of which knew the patient had been stockpiling them. Only his friends knew. It took weeks of counseling to quell their consciences as to whether "snitching" might have saved Tim's life. It could have, we agreed, but no one can control another man's sobriety or relapse.

The Rousting

Like ducks in an arcade shooting game, staffers were eliminated with steady precision. Keri, the recreation therapist, was moved upstairs to work with the high-rent veterans. She was not replaced. This was a huge loss for the vets, and it made no sense, since recreation therapy has tremendous healing benefits, especially for young returnees. Surfing, like many challenging outdoor activities, helps mitigate stress and tension for those reluctant to engage in traditional group therapy. The men of Cal Vet loved their trips to Knott's Berry Farm, to horse farms for equine therapy, and to bowling alleys. Now they spent their days slumped on sofas watching TV, which did nothing to boost their moods.

The transitional housing staff grew progressively smaller. The floor nurse was transferred upstairs. Many weeks, her replacement came downstairs to visit just once, for meetings. That's why when Jim stopped me in the hallway to say he felt dizzy and couldn't sleep—a seventy-seven-year-old schizophrenic who claimed to have been married to famed 1940s–50s dancer Cyd Charisse—I had to call upstairs for help. Said the new nurse, sounding startled by my call: "In emergencies, we aren't supposed to touch those people!" An hour later, an ambulance reserved for non-urgent cases picked up the elderly gentleman, brought him to the ER, where he was treated for a virus, then brought him back to his Cal Vet home.

Each week, it became more obvious: The state never wanted the feds on their property, hadn't adjusted to the idea over close to two years, was trying hard to push us out, and most certainly wouldn't devote precious state resources to help it succeed. It was more like they were helping it fail.

They even tried to scare people away. Veterans complained of being ambushed in the hall and told, "You have to get out of here soon!" I understood the Cal Vet point of view—so did the vets—that the home was intended to be transitional, not permanent housing, and residents were staying too long, languishing without plans, but pressure tactics like this have no place in a therapeutic environment. There's a more humane and constructive way to emphasize the need to move on rather than become all too comfortable on the government dole. Besides, was it the veterans' fault that affordable housing vouchers periodically dried up? Or that it took years to be awarded VA benefits due to the infamous backlog of cases? Or that they couldn't find jobs? There were solid reasons behind their lengthy stays. Most were not "those people," the lazy good-for-nothings.

I hadn't prepared to fight the state, but I also wasn't about to watch these vets "circle the drain" (a doctors' phrase for patients whose deaths are prolonged, circuitous and seem to dwindle down into infinity). My guys deserved better. They were still "with it" (relatively speaking), able-bodied (for the most part) and of sound mind (when on medications), but they had lost confidence and hope. I'm no orator, but my goal was, to quote the Reverend Jesse Jackson's failed but moving 1998 presidential campaign slogan, "Keep hope alive."

To start, I reinvented my Domiciliary "Straight Talk" group. This time, instead of discussions on national news, we focused solely on our plight at Cal Vet: What's going on with the state? Why doesn't the VA intervene to support its veterans? How can we improve this acrimonious marriage of the state and the feds? With the help of the "patient president"—he was motivated to keep the program intact, given his neck, back, skin, mental health, vocational, housing, alcohol and pain problems—we decided to hold monthly meetings at Cal Vet, at night, when state staff had gone home.

What was our mission? To strengthen the federal program. Assert our VA rights. Empower veterans. Report violations perpetrated by the state to the veterans' Congressman. Get the Congressman to pressure the state for better care. Reserve the right for vets to remain at Cal Vet until safe housing could be found. For everyone. However long it takes.

Nevertheless, Cal Vet continued down the warpath. One day, without warning, discharge letters with exit dates were dropped onto veterans' beds, like eviction notices from a bank. Panic ensued: "Really?" "I have to go to the street?" "Is there any way you can convince them to let me stay?"

In addition, there were gross privacy violations. One morning, the ground floor walls were plastered with rosters listing: veterans' names, discharge dates and Social Security numbers—illegal, per California privacy law, known as HIPAA (the Health Insurance Portability and Accountability Act). Immediately, I tore the lists down. No state staffer admitted to posting them.

At our first nighttime meeting, we were nearly forty strong, spread throughout the "C" lounge area just off the main lobby, with its gleaming marble floors, walls bedecked with military flags and framed photos of famous war scenes. The guys were scattered about on chairs, sofas, the floor, table tops, leaning against the glass wall in the back of the lobby, or peering through the glass from outside, in the courtyard where they smoked. Even the dozen or so vets returning "home" from work lingered, still in their work uniforms and suits (the latter supplied by vocational rehabilitation services).

But as we gained strength, so did the opposition. State staffers were recruited to serve as spies. Eddy from Nigeria, head of the ground floor, suddenly—suspiciously—started working late, just on Wednesday nights, once a month, when he knew we were scheduled to meet. Eddy's office was unnervingly close to the "C" lounge area. He could hear everything that was said. Likewise, Francisco, who cleaned and serviced all household appliances and supervised the crew responsible for vacuuming, mopping and garbage dumping, took to cleaning the "C" lobby refrigerator and microwave—also at 6:30 p.m., exactly when our meetings began. Once, an elderly Vietnam veteran who knew a thing or two about opposition forces pulled me aside before the meeting to whisper, "Get him out of here, he's on the state's side." He pointed to Francisco. "Why not first do lobbies A, B and D, which were empty?" he asked.

Good point. Me? I hadn't a clue at first, but when I asked Francisco to leave, he did.

I enjoyed rallying the troops. It was energizing, and it helped calm the vets' nerves, but within a few months attendance slacked off. Some of the vets had been scared into moving out, others sank back into lethargy and quiet despair.

Meanwhile the state proceeded apace, running roughshod.

Countdown

We had just concluded "treatment team." These were weekly sessions at which state staffers, myself and, sometimes, those few federal VA people on loan for the day (vocational rehabilitation, addiction therapy) met as a group with individual patients, at fifteen-minute intervals, to review their progress and readiness for discharge.

We set up shop in a make-shift Cal Vet office that doubled as a storage area for spare clothes (other rooms were reserved for more important, state-sponsored events). Surrounded by racks of second-hand men's interview suits, each vet was individually called in. Each sat on a folding chair directly across from us, the staffers, seated comfortably in recliners. Each would later say to me, in private, "It felt like a firing squad."

This particular Thursday morning, like every other Thursday morning, we went through the motions of our usual routine:

Eddy from Nigeria, looking regal in his high-backed recliner, legs crossed, hands neatly folded as if holding court: "Any complaints about your room?" Almost invariably, each vet said no. Later, in private, they would say, "Why talk? He doesn't do anything no matter what we report!"

Joseph from Korea, eager to please his bosses by increasing discharge numbers: "What eees youw tleatment pran?" with each vet asking me to translate his unique blend of Korean-infused English.

Sarah, the wispy dietician who ate berries for breakfast: "How is your weight?"—each vet answering with a sigh and a belly pat.

Susan, the nurse: "Let me know if you need anything."

Ken, the vocational rehabilitation specialist: "Hey man, forget about all those super skills and clerical stuff. You need a job, now. I've got someone who wants thirty vets to work railroad construction. Tomorrow!"

Jerry, the addiction therapist, old-school and hardline, who wore his Vietnam service like a bullet-proof vest: "I'm a veteran! I get it! Talk to me, not them!" Then even Joseph from Korea broke his silence: "Me too! I'm a veteran! In my countly, weec have mandatoly service!"

These meetings had become totally pointless. But as they were mandated by both state and federal governments, we carried on.

The Short Goodbye

There is a saying in recovery: "You know when you know." You either get it, or you don't. You've been there, or you haven't. Suddenly, deep personal conviction, long held in abeyance, breaks through your defenses to stage a surprise attack.

I knew after that treatment team meeting that I had to escape. I could weather chaos, unfairness, bigotry, excessive bureaucracy… but not uselessness. And not a lack of caring.

My hands were tied. I was outnumbered and overpowered by representatives of the state. And my employer, the VA, failed to lend a helping hand, to me and to the veterans.

At the same time, I had just learned that some of the state workers were sleeping in beds on the fourth floor of Cal Vet, Mondays through Fridays, to avoid long LA freeway commutes. This was entirely unethical. How could paid employees sleep in a building reserved for veterans? Including some who were homeless? No, those executive suites were not reserved for veterans, so the workers were not actually stealing veterans' beds. But surely, that space could have been used for veterans!

Not to mention the terrible optics. Steven, a graduate of the Domiciliary and a recovering alcoholic, described the scene: "They come in here Monday mornings, pulling suitcases on wheels, ready to get comfortable for the week." That had to hurt!

Besides, veterans like Steven—in fact, all those in permanent housing above the ground floor—paid a handsome rent, up to $1000 per month, or more, while the state staff paid ten dollars a night.

You know when you know. I was done. It was time to go, to jump ship, with the same speed and determination that once propelled me from the Domiciliary to Cal Vet.

I telephoned the Chief of the Domiciliary. "At what point does one become complicit?" I asked. "I can't go to the grave looking the other way." She knew what I meant: If forced to stay at Cal Vet, I would have to speak up about practices that seemed unethical. Truth-telling at the VA could be perilous, she knew—for her as well as me—so she arranged for my immediate transfer to the Welcome Center, across the parking lot.

The Welcome Center was yet another new VA venue, but in an old building— #257, a stucco structure, catty-corner and across the parking lot from the gleaming facade of the Cal Vet state home. Indeed, it was an eyesore. The Welcome Center was known as a homeless access center, a veterans' clearing house, a first stop for guys coming in directly off the streets every day, needing referrals for housing, benefits, the whole gamut of VA services.

Would the Welcome Center be a more caring therapeutic environment than Cal Vet? Who knew? But social workers were desperately needed there. The bulk of the staff consisted of paraprofessionals (vets on staff, not trained clinicians). So that weekend I

packed up, loaded my belongings into my car and left the following
note on my office door:

> *To the Veterans of THP:*
>
> *This is no way to say goodbye. But I want you to
> know that, effective Monday, I will no longer work
> here. Instead, I will be at the Welcome Center
> just across the parking lot. I am sorry that this has
> happened so fast and without prior notice, but it was
> necessary.*
>
> *I will always cherish the privilege and honor of
> working side by side with you, the fine gentlemen—
> and gentlewomen—of Cal Vet. I admire you all. I
> hope to still see you and invite you to visit me at my
> new place of work.*
>
> *With fondness and some sorrow,*
> *Andrea Plate, LCSW*

Within about a year, the program was shut down.

Chapter Nine

STRAIGHT OUTTA THE STREETS

Wikipedia, on the children's game, Pick-up Stix:

"The object of the game is to pick up the most sticks. To begin the game, a bundle of sticks is somewhat randomly distributed so that they end up in a tangled pile. The more tangled the resulting (dis)array, the more challenging the game."

A perfect encapsulated description of the VA Welcome Center.

If you build it, they will come. For housing. Food. TV. Coffee. Bathrooms. Showers. Laundry machines. Couches. Hygiene kits. Chill space in the dayroom. Et cetera.

They will come in all manner of altered states: Drunk. Stoned. Jaw-grinding on meth. Nodding off on heroin. Staggering. Angry. Psychotic. Hallucinating. Violent. Yelling. Scratching scabies. Scratching head lice. Running from the law.

When it opened in 2015, the Welcome Center was touted as a one-stop shop for homeless veterans. In the words of the Veterans Health Administration's National Center on Homelessness, it was envisioned as "a dignified place to stay while VA works to place them [veterans] in permanent housing as quickly as possible." This was not a housing facility. In fact, there were only thirty beds. It was more like a jam-packed traffic intersection for homeless veterans who didn't own cars.

To me, it represented something else—a late-stage surge, a last-ditch effort to end homelessness before President Obama's end of term in 2016. Thus, $540,000 was awarded to People Assisting the

Homeless, a community nonprofit partnering with the VA to provide additional outreach and emergency housing services. Almost
five million was given to the Salvation Army-run program, called
New Directions, which had its own veterans' treatment program
elsewhere on VA grounds, but was given a new task at the Welcome
Center: overseeing thirty beds and case managing the veterans occu-
pying them until they could be moved out. Suddenly, there was new
money—a good thing, sure, but how it's managed makes all the
difference—and the Welcome Center was a mess.

My colleagues at the Dom and Cal Vet responded in shock
when I announced my move: "It's crazy up there!" "Are you kidding?" "Are you really okay with that?" "I would never do that!"

No wonder. The Welcome Center was known as an extremely
chaotic, high-pressure, even dangerous place, with a steady flow,
daily, of the highest-risk veterans—drugged, intoxicated, imminently suicidal, imminently homicidal, even gravely disabled, both
mentally and physically. On my first day, a senior social worker
showing me around—she did not work there, and made a point
of telling me that—asked, in an intensely cautionary tone: "Do
you know how many social workers have come and gone through
these doors?" (Fortunately, I did not.) "It can be very scary to talk
to someone actively psychotic, hallucinating, and you don't know
what to do with him." Then she squelched a worker's idea to put me
behind the front desk so as to "get a feel for the place."

"No! Don't do that to Andrea!"

Some mornings, we called the VA police twice before 10:00
a.m. What else could we do? The Welcome Center was like the
Army without guns; the Navy without ships; the Marines without
muscle. There was no on-site MD; no psychiatrist; no psychologist; no addiction therapist; a dwindling number of social workers
(none before I got there); and one nurse, who came on board about
a month later.

Most of the staff were "peer support," in keeping with the D.C.-favored model of "veterans helping veterans." These young guys were passionate, well-meaning and unstoppable, but they couldn't possibly stem the overflowing tide of veterans. Who could? Nor should they, given liability concerns: If someone were to die, what would be the institution's defense? That an unlicensed person in recovery managed the case? That an imminently suicidal person was referred to a fellow veteran rather than a mental health clinician? This was wrong and unsafe—for everyone.

Vet-to-Vet

Mario was a peer counselor who had served in Iraq. A full-time employee, he was avidly engaged in treatment for PTSD and alluded to medical problems he chose not to disclose. Mario didn't talk about his time in the Marines. He didn't want to. From day one, though, it was obvious that the military had shaken him somehow. He was edgy and hyperactive, rushing up and down the halls all day, eager to cure every single ill of every veteran wandering in. He would engage them in long, heartfelt, vet-to-vet individual sessions, frequently punctuated by hugs, reassuring pats on the back, and the refrain: "I know, man. I'm a vet. I've been there."

This worried me. Mario was well-meaning, of course; but should a veteran in the throes of his own PTSD treatment be counseling a patient much like himself? Every day Mario would shepherd the most highly distressed and vulnerable young returnees into a tiny, cramped office just off the lobby—the one you couldn't miss, directly to the right of the front desk when you came in—then close the office door. What were two traumatized veterans doing in there, without clinical supervision?

Around 1:20 p.m. one Friday afternoon, the door burst open. Mario emerged. He was sobbing, hyperventilating, gasping for air. His face was red. His fists were clenched. For a few seconds, he couldn't speak. Then he erupted: "I can't!" (gasp). "I can't, I can't, I—I—I"—Mario turned and exited the building, ran down the stairs outside to his car and, I later learned, drove home. (He was "okay" Monday morning. Per staff, he frequently had panic attacks.)

I peered into the little office. There sat the abandoned patient, a twenty-something, burly white guy, in the chair opposite Mario's empty desk. Recently back from Afghanistan, he didn't seem fazed by Mario's behavior. Then a moment later, another peer support worker popped up behind me in the doorway—a very tall guy, peering over my shoulder. This was "Sweetie," so nicknamed because his last name was "Sweet"—a thin, African American Vietnam combat veteran who received maximum disability payments for severe PTSD.

"What's going on, brother?" he asked. Without another word, Sweetie gently moved me aside, stepped into the office and shut the door.

It was scenes like these that prompted top brass to command social workers to the Welcome Center. But with no organizational plan or chart, there was in fact no organization. It was a game of Pick-up Stix—see where things fall. Come what may.

Ready or Not

Obviously, the mission of the Welcome Center was to welcome everyone. Or was it? Debates raged between two opposing camps that believed:

(1) "Everyone deserves a chance," and
(2) "I deserve to work in a safe environment."

These arguments surfaced every day, when we were confronted with cases like these: A hospital escapee trailing a catheter under his gown (he wanted housing); a man banned from the ER after trying to strangle a nurse; a sixty-year-old with a psychotic disorder, blind in one eye, racing down the halls and rattling doorknobs while crying, "Help!" (then denying whatever help was offered); a would-be rapper who whispered "baby," "sugar," "sweetheart," "darlin'" or "sexy lady," never more than three inches from a woman's face; a vet who had served in Iraq, shouting obscenities, then videotaping the ensuing chaos for "the Congressman" or "TV news"; an old guy suffering from pain and marijuana addiction, smoking pot in the bathroom.

How did these veterans find their way here? Some followed the signs on campus, saying "Welcome Center," with arrows pointing uphill. Some were "dumped" by social workers who didn't, or couldn't, come up with a viable discharge plan for their veterans. Some were sent from the VA's main hospital, after days if not weeks on the hospital's medical or psychiatric wards, until doctors finally ordered them "out, today!"

Clearly, what some patients needed, we didn't have. Those who showed up at the Welcome Center needing acute care—hallucinating, in the throes of delirium tremens, imminently suicidal—would be immediately transported to the ER. But in all too many cases they returned, later that same day—especially the mentally ill who were deemed "unholdable"—meaning, they were not sufficiently gravely disabled to warrant involuntary admission to a psychiatric ward. Evaluated and released, they would return to request housing, usually when all beds at the VA or in programs around town were filled.

In addition to the thirty beds supervised by New Directions staff, there were military cots—for a while. These were opened on the floor of the dayroom, just past the lobby. During work hours, it was a different scene: Veterans would hunker down on tattered couches, folding chairs or the thinly carpeted floor, where they would sleep, watch the widescreen TV, charge their cell phones

(yes—every veteran had a cell phone!) or simply stare ahead, waiting for a social worker to call them for a one-on-one appointment
to discuss housing. The greatest attraction was a coffee pot that
looked like an artifact from the medical center's opening in 1887.
But hot Folger's in a styrofoam cup goes a long way for someone
who's homeless.

After 6:00 p.m., the scene would change (I rarely stuck around
to see it, though—eight hours on the job was enough!). Then, the
dayroom would become a communal bedroom. Twenty military
cots would be unfolded across the floor. Veterans would vie for spots
on the cots. Each night, a lucky twenty veterans would sleep there.
Staff would awaken them around 6:00 a.m. to fold and stash the
cots away. These were highly coveted cots—twenty spots in which
to sleep, undisturbed by case managers or program demands.

But even the cots came at a cost: Weren't we social workers
supposed to eliminate homelessness, rather than encourage it? Why
were dozens choosing to sleep on the floor rather than in community programs? Accordingly, we tried to implement restrictive
criteria (for example, cots reserved only for those veterans with very
specific needs, like a one-night stay prior to the next day's surgery, or
a veteran arriving late in the afternoon from out of state).

What stood in our way was the vets on staff. They didn't care
about statistics. They cared about getting vets off the streets and into
beds. Every night. Thus, they struck private deals, promising cots to
guys after "regular staff" like me went home.

The Welcome Center had no flood insurance for the sea of vets
pouring in. Or, as an administrator put it, "We're afraid someone
will die inside." Of course. Guys were shooting up, staggering in
drunk, twitching from meth-induced sleep-deprivation and paranoia. Within months, the cots were removed. Word from above was,
"Get them into housing!"

The Stench of Homelessness

I have never known hunger (aside from dieting), but Ricardo had. He was a small, elfin man, a former Army guy with enormous energy, stationed at the front desk of the Welcome Center. He could stop any veteran's rant by asking, "Hungry? Want something to eat?" Tensions ran high when the food ran out, even though only snacks were offered, like Cup-a-Soup or granola bars. When a hefty veteran once asked me, "Got any hamburgers?" I knew it was his first visit.

There was a shower room. I don't how many stalls it had, or what the room looked like; women (both vets and staff) were shut out. Female veterans were instead escorted to the clinic upstairs, which also had showers. Female escorts—a nurse, a female peer technician from the Welcome Center—were made to stand guard outside the door upstairs while the veteran cleaned herself up (social workers were spared this task).

Still, I was spared neither the sights nor sounds of the men's-only shower room. My office, situated just a few doors away and down a long, poorly lit hallway, put me smack in the center of puddles, clomping feet, soggy, hairy chests pressed against wife-beater shirts, and, in one memorable instance, a large, fleshy, freshly showered guy pushing his wheelchair, nude except for a washcloth on his lap.

The shower system was supposed to be orderly: A sign-in sheet. Services rendered on a first-come, first-served basis. Hours of operation, roughly 8:30 to 11:30 a.m. All men escorted by male staff (you simply cannot have men who are intoxicated, stoned, hungry, mentally ill, psychotic or disabled ambling independently down the hall).

There were slip-ups, though. One morning a family of four, including two small children, was discovered showering alongside men in adjacent stalls.

The beleaguered dad pleaded the family's case: For weeks, the parents and two kids had been sleeping in their van. But now, caught sneaking in, they were punished. The veteran was banned from the Welcome Center for a month, while his family was told never to come back. Nude children and adult men side by side! Imagine the potential for child abuse and liability!

Sometimes, signs were posted on the entryway and outside the building: "Laundry room and showers closed today due to staffing shortages." A shower shut-down! Services denied! This not only *was* bad, it looked bad. No top administrator or politician could know. Accordingly, when staff from the VA Secretary's office came to visit for the day, the signs were taken down (then put back up). This happened more than once. The "no shower" signs were also removed the day of LA's famed annual runners' Marathon. One part of the route ran right through the West LA VA campus, past the Welcome Center. Why alert runners to the reality of suspended service? No doubt some of those marathoners were well-heeled professionals, voters and campaign contributors.

Whenever the showers were shut off, it was best to avoid the dayroom. Although the odor was foul, the use of aerosols was forbidden due to fear of insulting the veterans. (Never mind the poor vets huddled there with all sorts of contagion, uncleanliness and lack of ventilation.)

Families Have Children

Most of the programs were for single male veterans. Nevertheless toddlers, teens, babies and nursing mothers frequently came in. It was dreadful. "Sorry, we don't have placements for families," I would say, before referring them to community services; but there were not many, the demand was overwhelming, and those services were "not officially recommended" by the VA—for liability reasons, it was imperative to add that.

Otherwise, I could only direct families to call 211, the LA County seven-day-a-week homeless hotline for emergency assistance. Most of those families had already done so, which is why they came to the Welcome Center.

The children were remarkable—quiet, polite, cooperative, undemanding—as if tranquilized or anesthetized. Had they been bounced around so much they couldn't feel the bumps? Were they afraid to aggravate parents who were already stressed out? I don't know. But these families appeared to be close-knit, with everyone playing carefully crafted roles: Moms watching kids; dads asking questions; parents conferring; kids waiting patiently for snacks (accepting none without parental approval!). They were determined to stay together, even if that meant sleeping in a van outside the kids' schools.

It was the irresponsible parents I couldn't bear. Fortunately, there weren't many, because they wouldn't have bothered to come to our doors. One memorable morning, however, a woman veteran walked in with two little boys, ages 4 and 6, one holding each hand. She told us that she found them in a parking lot, outside, in a locked car. Inadvertently, they had set off the car alarm. She persuaded them to open the door, then brought them to the Welcome Center. They were waiting for their father, the little boys explained. He had "an appointment" at the hospital across the way and had told them to wait.

First, we called the VAPD, then took turns babysitting until the cops arrived. In that time, we learned a few things: (1) that the older brother wanted to be a fireman; and (2) their father's full name. With that, the police located the dad by phone, summoned him to the Welcome Center and, I was told hours later, upbraided him for leaving two small children inside a locked car. Reportedly, he responded, "What's wrong with that?" Then the VAPD called Child Protective Services.

A Waitlist for Transgender Veterans

Few programs will admit transgender veterans because they lack the resources and ingenuity to manage these complex cases. Services cannot be denied, but they can be delayed. I once waited a month for a transgender veteran to be afforded a Domiciliary bed.

This was John, a handsome, soft-spoken, thirty-year-old African American veteran, fully transitioned from female to male, whose gorgeous eyes—milk chocolate in color, large and luminous, rimmed by curled lashes—sparked my envy. You couldn't help but notice. I offered my empathic best, saying, "I know the gender issue is hard for you," but he nabbed me on that: "It's not! I'm perfectly comfortable with who I am, but I need a room!" A month after his acceptance, still with no available single rooms (post–J-Hi, all transgender veterans got single rooms), I appealed to the Domiciliary Chief, who normally doesn't get involved in admissions decisions. "Can we really put off such a hot-button political case?" I asked. The next day, Domiciliary administrators "found" a room for my guy by moving an emotionally disturbed veteran from a single room into a two-man room. Alas, overnight, John left the program—or, to use VA/military-speak—went AWOL. Remember, these VA programs have watchmen but no police or trained guards, and it is against policy to force a veteran to stay in treatment if he is not gravely disabled. I could only hope the troubled vet made to vacate his single room at the Domiciliary was permitted to move back in.

Once, this past year, when describing this sad state of affairs to a political science class at Loyola Marymount University, here in Los Angeles, I asked students to participate in a debate on the right of transgender persons to serve in the military. One young woman from Thailand seemed annoyed: "What's the big deal? It seems kind of silly. In my country, we have trans people and lady boys. They're just part of society."

Good question. What's the big deal?

Less Than Honorable

Not every veteran who separates from the Service gets the designation of "honorable." Some are labeled "OTH," for "Other Than Honorable"—better than "dishonorable" but far worse than "honorable." In practice, vets with OTH status have limited eligibility for services, on two grounds that I know of: (1) They served in the military a short period of time (less than two years); or (2) they were convicted of some legal infraction (including possession of marijuana). OTH veterans qualify for a single benefit: transitional housing in the community—definitely not the Domiciliary, or anywhere on federal government property! But even community programs reserve the right to deny admission to OTH vets. Furthermore, *all* OTHs are denied *all* medical care at the VA. They cannot even go to the VA lab to take the TB test required for admission to a community program. Instead, they have to find a private or nonprofit community clinic. Many veterans left to take the tests but never returned. It must have been so much easier to get high again.

Homeowners Who Feel Homeless

Homeless programs will not accept needy veterans who have homes. This makes sense, until you think about it. What happens to the veteran with a home who needs treatment for a substance abuse or mental health disorder? I remember one man crying, "It's not safe! There's all these drugs where I live. There's the dealer. I need to get out of there!" No matter. Said the social worker to whom I was trying to refer the guy, over the phone: "On the books, he's not homeless." Eventually, this man was housed in a program, but I have no doubt that he continued to use drugs up to his admission date.

Sex Offenders on the Streets

It was a great challenge to work with sex offenders. Where could they be referred? Sex offenders were banned from community agencies, sober livings, nearly all VA-contracted community programs, and residential placements on VA grounds—except, once again, the fully federally funded Domiciliary. But there was a backlog of applications for Domiciliary admission. Where would the sex offender live while waitlisted for an admissions interview, then a bed?

I had one chronically homeless man, age fifty-six, who bemoaned his fate: "I touched an underaged girl thirty years ago and I'm still paying the price!" I could see his point; but I could also see the mother's point, and the girl's point. Every day the sex offender returned to the Welcome Center, hoping, he said, for "a miracle" (read: a place to sleep). After a month, he stopped coming by.

I remember, too, the middle-aged Hispanic man, guilty of a sex offense going back just a few years, who arrived with an entourage: his mother, sister and wife, all of whom loved him and wanted him to stay in the home they shared. But this would violate the law. Instead, he hung out every day at the Welcome Center, then slept overnight under a tree. Within a month he had a bed in the Domiciliary.

No Failsafe

"Go to your office and lock the door!" a staff member shouted when one particularly disruptive vet, banned from other VA sites, plunged into a violent rant. But the door couldn't be locked from the inside, and I had no key. For months, I petitioned for a key, but one locksmith manufactured keys for all 127,000 healthcare employees, and one police station distributed them. Following procedure, I didn't expect to get one anytime soon. So on May 31, 2016, I sent the following email to the Chief of Police:

As a VA social worker who has been on campus fourteen years I am well aware of how congested the system is and the myriad competing needs of staff.

However, I am now working at building 257, the Welcome Center, which is a walk-in center for the homeless. It is a high-acuity station. Veterans come in off the street who are under the influence, prone to violence, etc. I know that it is more acute here; I worked 12.5 years at the Dom; one year at Cal Vet; and now in building 257.

I have not had an office key for five weeks, since transferring here. The process is stalled, like so many others.

But this is NOT a place like so many others.

Furthermore, the door of my office, room 125A, does not lock and has no lock capability.

Last week, when a potentially dangerous veteran entered the premises, I was told to go in my room and lock the door, then stay inside. I could not do as I was told.

Is this really all we can do? Isn't this rather dangerous?

Please assist in this matter if at all possible. I have tried, to no avail.

I do indeed value my life.

Thank you,
Andrea Plate

The Chief of Police did not respond. A few weeks later, two workmen, sent by some department, somewhere, at the request of some department head, somewhere—I played no part in this—came to my Welcome Center office with a toolbox, to fix an overhead cabinet that had come unhinged. "It could fall on your head!" one exclaimed. I hadn't noticed, nor had I asked them to come, but I knew that rare good VA thing when I saw it, so I proposed, "If you fix something I don't care about, can you fix something I really need?" An hour later, the lock was installed (no work order, no paper trail). They felt sorry for me. Said one of them: "Sure, hon', it's a rough place."

The Welcome Center had one security guard under contract to a private firm. One. He did his best to stop angry and impetuous veterans from traipsing down the hall, to intervene in fights between vets, and to tamp down verbal assaults on staff, like: "I ain't taking no orders from a female!" and "You deny me services, and we'll take it outside…"

Unfortunately, the guard was ordered to cease and desist. In the event of impending danger, he was told, he must alert the VA police rather than himself intervene. Given this, I never again confronted excessively upset veterans inside my office; it was safer and smarter to vacate and move into a high-visibility area. Sometimes it took time for other staff to coax an angry veteran from my office. But I figured, better to lose my wallet than my life.

The nicer guys—those veterans watching quietly from the sidelines while waiting for appointments, housing applications, snacks, a fresh batch of coffee—responded in kind. They wanted to protect and defend. Kill the enemy. Save a damsel in distress. However sorely tempted, I never accepted one of their offers to punch a bully on my behalf.

Attack with an Undeadly Weapon

At the Welcome Center, things never got off to a slow start. Each day was like riding bumper cars at an amusement park. Lurch forward. Stop fast. Back up. To the right. No, the left! Careening down

the hallways, you never knew what lay ahead. Among my clear-
est memories: A young vet who had served in Iraq, gyrating in a
drug-induced trance to a tune only he could hear or a wind only he
could feel, his skinny frame twisting into tai-chi-like curves. (Who
cares, said staff?! He's not hurting anybody!) Or the six-foot-six
African American man built like a telephone pole, decked out in a
jacket with aluminum foil fringes and a hat decorated with stickers
of the Stars and Stripes, who fancied himself Stevie Wonder's cousin
(and got us all to sign Stevie's deluxe-size birthday card). Or the
male-to-female transgender veteran known as Cherry, in oversized,
floppy sweaters and pajama pants; although slim and short, she had
a giant pair of lungs: "Excuse me, rude people! I want housing! Do
your job!" Or the pale, frail elderly man in a wheelchair, draped in
blankets despite the 75-degree spring air, gasping from emphysema
and in search of an oxygen tank.

This day was no different. Vets streamed in, asking for, and
demanding: housing, food, coffee, job leads, cigarettes... A particularly anxious-looking veteran, obviously a newbie, flagged me down:
"Can I get housing here? Are you a social worker?" Overwhelmed,
I sought refuge back at my desk, but almost immediately the lone
security guard up front came to my office. He looked hesitant,
almost shy. "Mrs. Plate," he said in a whisper, although no one was
within earshot. "Did you know that man was taking pictures with a
cell phone up your skirt?" No, I did not. I vaguely remembered the
feel of something cold, maybe metallic, on my leg above the knee,
but until he said this it hadn't entered my mind. "You have to file a
report!" the guard said. "Call the police!" A few others on staff said
the same.

No, I didn't want to do that. Vulgar sexist language was an
everyday affair in this line of work. Who cares about a quick grope?

Instead, and without consultation, someone else on staff called,
probably the guard. Soon two VAPD officers swaggered into my

office, hands on hips, faces etched in official concern (penetrating eye-to-eye looks; stiff, excessively solicitous smiles). They were there "to investigate," they said. What did I actually see, or feel? I was not forthcoming. It didn't seem like a big deal, or at least that's how I wanted it to seem; and I wanted them to go away. Four men crowded around my desk—the security guard, an eyewitness from the New Directions program, plus two cops. It was really embarrassing. They insisted—all four of these guys—on viewing the surveillance video (I rejected their invitation to come along and watch). The cops then reported back to me, saying, in the most solemn of tones, that they "could not see direct contact... a passerby blocked our view." Were they disappointed? Had they hoped for their own sneak peek? (They did in fact confiscate the vet's cell phone, photos and all). They went on to console me by saying that they had spoken to the vet, who was very sorry. No, I didn't want to press charges, thank you. Finally, they left.

What followed was a feminist fusillade from the Welcome Center program director, another social worker, and two VA Supported Housing staffers:

"Why didn't you press charges?"

"That's sexual harassment!"

"All day you advocate for veterans, then don't defend yourself?"

"What if it happens to someone else??"

All legitimate points, but a little like closing the barn door after the horse is out. Such were the entreaties of my colleagues, but I would not be moved, and for good reason: James was a big, bulky forty-something African American guy with a history of childhood trauma and TBI (traumatic brain injury), the latter sustained in a motorcycle crash. He struggled with coordination and balance. He swayed when he first stood, and suffered extreme moods swings, from anxiety to depression. He had learned some coping strategies to manage his moods. These included clenching his fists and grunting (rather than verbalizing frustration and anger). But these mannerisms spooked people, who avoided him or felt provoked to fight. Accordingly, he had been tossed out of multiple programs.

Who was worse off, then? Me, with a cell phone slipped up my Marc Jacobs skirt? Or James, permanently and severely disabled? As for personal safety, why anger the guy by filing charges? Surely that would hinder, if not terminate, his housing applications. Who's to say that, in an act of revenge, he wouldn't stake out the parking lot and slash me with a knife when I left work, or follow me in his car? Hysteria? No. A grip on reality.

Whatever. It was my skirt, my body. The case was dropped, and with it, the level of esteem with which I was regarded by my feminist colleagues dropped as well.

Over and Out

The large, gymnasium-like dayroom, dark and dingy, standing-room only, was somber and still on Inauguration Day. No one complained that the ancient coffee pot had run out of Folger's, or that the wait to see a social worker was too long. The veterans were riveted to the TV. Silence ruled the roost as Donald J. Trump was sworn in. Then suddenly, one man jumped to his feet, yelling (to no one in particular), "I'm not gonna listen to that guy Trump!"

Said another, sneering cynically: "Well, I am! I wanna watch everything he does! I'm gonna keep track of every move."

In the lobby, an older veteran, seemingly weary but good-humored, seated on a well-worn, fake-leather couch, pointed to the empty spot on the wall from which Barack Obama's portrait had been removed, on official orders, before noon: "Am I really gonna have to look at Donald Trump's picture up there?!" He shook his head and laughed.

None of us talked politics that day, but many of us, both patients and staff, were downcast. It helped when a longtime recovering addict and champion of vets, now working as a vocational rehab counselor, tried to console us: "As long as it doesn't hurt the vets I don't care," he said. "And I don't think it will."

Of course, we had no idea that within fourteen months, two VA secretaries would come and go. Obama's man, Secretary Robert McDonald, was sacked just after Trump's inauguration. The new president promoted David Shulkin, McDonald's deputy, to the top job. Then Shulkin resigned. The White House attributed this to Shulkin's ethics violation scandals. Shulkin's story was that the Trump Mafia scapegoated him for opposing privatization of the VA. Next, Ronny Jackson, former Presidential Physician (for both "W" and Obama), was nominated for the position, but withdrew his name amidst a flurry of allegations that included excessive drinking on the job, maintaining a hostile work environment and distributing non-prescribed narcotics to staff on overseas trips. Just what the VA needs! The new VA Secretary is Robert Wilkie, a proponent of privatization.

Most of the vets I knew opposed privatization. They figured, what you see is what you get. In their minds, they got good medical and mental health care (however hard to access), from cutting-edge clinicians trained in veteran-specific treatment protocols for post-traumatic stress disorder and traumatic brain injury. What do physicians in private practice know about these? Not much. Despite myriad complaints and frustrations, most vets are willing to squeeze their way through the bloated bubble of VA bureaucracy to receive such specialized care. They may not trust the VA, but they trust the private sector even less.

Would a new administration be a game-changer? Or just another game of Pick-up Stix?

Chapter Ten

THE HEART OF THE MATTER:
LOOKING BACK

Social work students will ask, "How could you deal with so many hard cases, every day?" I'm always tempted to say, "Because I'm crazy. What 'normal' person would do this kind of work?" But as irony escapes the very young, I usually feign nonchalance by saying, "I've always liked Bad Boys," or "It's fun to walk on the wild side." No lie there. The question I get from people of all ages is, "What can you really do for these veterans?" My answer is, if a man who feels truly alone believes that I care about him; if a veteran tastes sobriety for just a week or two; or if he stays off the streets for a while—a few days, a week—it's worth it.

I grew attached to some of "my" veterans—not many, and not often—but intense emotion is one of the hazards of social work. Sometimes I found myself looking at a certain type—a young man recently returned from Iraq who couldn't sleep, couldn't concentrate, couldn't relate to his family and couldn't hear well (due to tinnitus, or ringing in the ears, from exposure to gunfire and other explosions). I would feel the urge to make him better—feed him, introduce him to friends… But feelings of this nature are unhealthy. They cloud your clinical objectivity. You have to be aware of them, then fight them off.

Bakersfield Blues

Age: Fifty-six. Race: Caucasian. Drug of choice: Alcohol.

To me, he would always be that tow-headed boy, age four, drunk on whiskey and passed out on the living room floor. His parents loved to "booze it up and shoot the shit," he explained, and sometimes, for extra fun, they would give him drinks so they could watch him wobble into the couch or fall to the floor.

This was Dan, one of my first veteran heroes—skinny and concave, with a spine like a backwards question mark, a toothless grin and hair greased into a dirty blond ponytail. Dan was from Bakersfield—a freeway exit on Interstate 405, as far as I knew—but the hometown of many vets who talked about its horse shows, drag races, and, of course, its bountiful supply of drugs. I also learned that in 2015, the American Lung Association rated it the number one city in the nation for pollution.

Dan chain-smoked, drank a lot, and had colon cancer. For four years, he ignored the stomach trouble until the doctor he finally saw said, "If you want to live, you have to stay clean." Thus, Dan sought treatment for alcohol abuse.

And yet he claimed that his other addiction, to sex, was worse.

I had heard this claim before, usually by men trying to be macho, but Dan was a textbook case of the real thing—exhausted by all the time and energy he spent pursuing sex, never feeling satiated and, therefore, unable to focus on much else. He explained it like this: After eight years of marriage, his wife left him for a man, so "I figured I wasn't good in bed." Deeply hurt, he set out to dispel this insecurity. His strategy was to rack up sexual conquests fueled by alcohol and crack. So he ended up with three addictions (crack, alcohol, and sex). Dan was a bit of a hustler, too. He claimed to run a prostitution ring in Bakersfield, on a freelance basis, for extra cash.

Dan needed a lifestyle overhaul. There is a time-worn recovery saying: "If you take the alcohol away from a drunken horse thief, what do you have? A horse thief." To get well, he needed to leave Bakersfield, his drug buddies, and the prostitution ring.

He succeeded for several months, faithfully attending therapy groups, staying clean and meeting with me for individual counseling. This was no sophisticated, psychodynamic intervention. Dan just needed a chance to talk about things he otherwise kept hidden: his failed marriage, the free sex he got from hookers, his pride in a well-run prostitution ring. He explained that he respected these women, some of whom were single mothers he helped stay financially afloat. He was equally respectful of me, precisely because of his sex addiction. He was well aware of his sexual impulsivity and didn't dare step out of bounds.

Unfortunately, Dan said he "got tempted" one night by some friends who drifted into town. For months, they had been calling from Bakersfield, begging him to come home. They wanted his help with the hooker business, but he didn't seem to care. So they drove to LA, checked into a nearby motel and invited him to "party."

Dan enjoyed himself, but a complication arose back at the VA Sunday morning: The breathalyzer he took registered 0.06- -a low level, to be sure, but higher than the "0" that, at the time, the program would tolerate. Dan claimed to have stayed sober all night but in the morning, while straightening up the room, he picked up a plastic cup half-filled with "gasoline champagne"—I took that to mean very cheap stuff—and drank it. Knowing he would be discharged, he was both mildly regretful and intensely proud that "at this age, I can still have that much sex, that many times in one night, and give women a good time." To my surprise, however, he requested a referral to another program. Was he trying to please me?

It was not easy. "Why should we take him now?" asked a social worker from another program. "He just failed. He's not ready."

Other referral sources stated similar beliefs, adding that "bad choices should have punishing consequences"—even short-term homelessness. It was 2004. "Tough love" was still in vogue, but these program gatekeepers had another concern. Dan was likely to relapse again—which would mean a "bad outcome" for the program. Too many bad outcomes can result in budget cuts.

By the day's end, however, I managed to find one place in Simi Valley that would take in the Bakersfield boy.

"Do they have parking?" he asked. By this time, I was miffed. The guy's life was on the line, and that was his concern?! Dan could read my face. "I have $1.19 in my pocket," he said. "My truck is all I have."

Point well-taken.

Later that afternoon, he left me a sweet and rambling phone message: "Hi, darlin'... I decided to go back to Bakersfield for the weekend... You're great at what you do, and I know you take it home with you when things don't work out." Twice he called me "hon," adding, "This is kind of, you know, not official... Like, just between you and me... Bye, darlin'. See ya Monday." Three hours, and he was already high. I was sure he wouldn't to return to LA, and I was right.

That was the end of my first veteran hero-crush. I missed Dan, but I wasn't discouraged. He'd come a long way from his days as a four-year-old drunk. He had shown me respect and restraint. He had learned that not all females are unfaithful wives or hookers. And he called to say, "Thank you." What's not to love?

The last I heard, he had not died of colon cancer, he had a girlfriend, and they were living together in a VA Supported Housing apartment in downtown Bakersfield.

From Manslaughter to Mainstream

He had me at "Hello." I had just finished reading "In the Place of Justice," by Walter Rideau, an ex-felon turned liberal cause célèbre after thirty years of incarceration in "Angola," Louisiana's notorious state prison, for murder. Now I was in the presence of another ex-felon with the potential to find redemption, fortune and fame. He had spent twenty-three years in an Arizona penitentiary and had been out only a year.

Jim was quirky, temperamental, and charming. Now fifty-three, he looked like a has-been surfer—tall, lanky, with straggly blond hair skimming his shoulders and flip-flops flapping the backs of his heels as he walked. A recovering crack addict, he downed two twelve-packs of Pepsi every day.

Jim had gotten off to a bad start in life. At age eleven, he was raped by an adult male in his Tucson neighborhood. At thirteen, he ran away from home to "pimp myself" to men across country. At sixteen, he was expelled from school for so many run-ins with authority that, decades later, he couldn't remember the nature of his transgressions.

Then at age twenty-three, "cracked out," he was convicted of manslaughter. Jim described the crime as a buddy thing. He and his friend, short-changed $300 worth of crack, set out for revenge against "the guy" who did the bad deed. Jim's friend beat up the guy, then Jim "finished him off" by holding his foot on the man's neck until he died. A day later, on a crack low, Jim turned himself in to authorities, and spent the next twenty-three years in a penitentiary. Once released, he decided to leave Arizona behind and start fresh somewhere else: The West LA Department of Veterans Affairs. So the homegrown Arizonian moved to California, which just happened to have the biggest VA healthcare facility nationwide.

Jim was sorry for the hurt his crime had caused his mother. She was the only person who regularly visited him behind bars. She was the only woman who loved him… except Amber, the prostitute he met at a gas station and with whom he had fallen in love—but that was years ago, before the manslaughter. Jim and Amber planned to get married, even though they never had sex. Jim was fine with that, happy to prove he wasn't like "every other guy." The plan failed when, one fateful morning at least twenty-five years ago, they inadvertently fumbled their way through "wake-up sex." The next morning, Amber was gone.

Jim's diagnosis was antisocial personality disorder. He had many of its trademark symptoms: a history of extensive violence, risk-taking and abusive relationships, coupled with that odd talent for "using charm or wit to manipulate others for personal gain or pleasure" (as stated in the Diagnostic and Statistical Manual of Mental Disorders, or DSM-V, used by clinicians). I admit, I was charmed. Jim had a mischievous smile and a funny way of tilting his head to the side while awaiting my reaction to his latest bombast. "You kill one guy and pay for it forever!" he moaned. "That's right," I said coldly. "That's the law." Then he attempted to soften his image by admitting that at times, from the corner of his eye, he still caught phantom glimpses of Alejandro, the drug dealer he had helped murder for doing him wrong. He mentioned the dead man's name just once, with a whisper, eyes shut.

Jim was resilient. He would not give up on himself. He was not one of those veterans who says, all too casually, "I want to turn my life around." He meant it, and although it was at first rough going—he was wild-tempered, like a feral cat—Jim calmed down and gained some trust in others. He even agreed to meet with me individually on a weekly basis. For Jim, this was a whole new form of communication: truthful talk based on trust. He in fact admitted that he loved "our talks," and that I was the only woman who cared about him besides his mother (what about Amber?).

For me, too, there was a thrill: Working with that rare, resilient ex-felon who actually thrives in long-term incarceration. He had made good use of those twenty-three years behind bars.

Upon program completion, Jim went to the Weingart transitional program. Compared to prison, Skid Row, that hub of homelessness and drugs in downtown LA, was no threat. He got a part-time job washing dishes. He walked five miles to and from work, six days a week. He saved enough money to buy an old car that frequently broke down, in which case he took the bus to his VA appointments. Here was a vet who stayed steady on psych meds, cooperated with his Weingart case manager and planned to enroll in baking school so as to update and enhance his work experience. Prior to prison, he had worked as a chef.

Throughout this time, Jim stayed in touch. He would stop by to see me when he came to the VA for mental health appointments. On Christmas, he gave me a card inscribed: "Thank you for all that you have done for me." Above all, he found humor where others found despair. We laughed together at his cell phone shot of a toilet paper roll, chained to the wall at Weingart, in case some desperate resident tried to steal it. "Life is good," he said, displaying the free backpack and socks handed out for the holidays on Skid Row. He was happy in that neighborhood. It felt like home. Every day he saw ghosts of his former self on the street—men and women, hard-up and high in this down-and-out concrete dungeon. Today, he was so much better!

Within about a year, Jim moved into a very low-cost HUD/VA Supportive Housing apartment.

I last saw him at a Domiciliary graduation. These could be tedious affairs. Twice-yearly, Domiciliary protocol was to stage a ceremony honoring every veteran who had completed the program. Each would be awarded a diploma. Vets and their families gathered in the Vets Gardens, a park area on VA grounds just across from the Dom and separated by an iron railing from the south side of Wilshire Boulevard. It was a lovely setting. There were benches tucked under the shade of quaint adobe overhangs, a fragrant rose garden and several small, bubbling waterfalls.

Unfortunately, many of the graduates failed to show up. This resulted in long, embarrassing periods of silence after their names were called. Those silences were a sort of public pronouncement signifying one of three things: the veteran was working, the veteran had moved, or the veteran had relapsed. No telling how many of each.

The end of the ceremony was "open mic time." Jim, in a surprise move, strode up front, took hold of the microphone and told the crowd how well he was doing in his apartment, and that he remained sober. Then he raised his head a notch above the microphone, quickly glanced at me on a folding chair just a few rows from the front, and said: "I want to thank Mrs. Plate, my social worker, and the full treatment team for all the help.'"

Moments like this kept me going fifteen years.

Listen Up!

He was determined to tune out the world. He wore white headphones, indoors and outdoors, all day, except in therapy groups.

Now in his forties, Allan, an ex-Navy man addicted to alcohol and crack, had never been sober more than six weeks, and never in an "uncontrolled environment" (which means living independently, instead of in a program or in jail). Of late, he had been acting like a "dry drunk"—cranky and irritable, struggling to make it through the day without Jack Daniels. One day, Allan got into a fierce argument with his roommate Graham—a "cool dude" with wavy, sandy-blond hair and chiseled features, nicknamed "Graham Cracker" because his home state was Tennessee and he "seemed racist." But Graham Cracker alone was not at fault. Allan liked to taunt him by saying, "What's a nice boy like you doing in a place like this?"

Late one morning. Allan appeared at my door to announce, "I'm leaving!" He couldn't stay at the Dom anymore, he said, due to tensions from the fight. Of note, he didn't ask for a new room assignment. He didn't want to discuss his decision. What he wanted to do was leave the program and get high—that was pretty obvious. I had a hunch, in fact, that he had provoked the fight to manufacture an excuse for getting drunk. That's why they call it "stinkin' thinkin'."

I knew better than to argue with a veteran craving alcohol or crack. Confrontation would worsen his mood and only reinforce his penchant for self-sabotage.

So at the conclusion of the rant, I told Allan I wasn't at all surprised he wanted to leave: "Six weeks is your longest time sober, ever," I said. "Time's up." He did not respond, so I went further: "Leave if you want, but be honest about why you're doing it." Was he listening? I couldn't tell, but it was worth one last try: "You told me you've been running away all your life. Has it helped?" Allan shrugged and left.

Hours later, he was back at my Domiciliary door. Why? What had happened?

"I was sitting on the bus and I heard your voice, Mrs. Plate," he said, at once relieved to be back in treatment but annoyed that I was "right." He explained his intentions: "I was gonna go somewhere, not sure where, but I kept hearing the last thing you said to me: 'You always run away.'" Two stops later, he hopped off the bus and headed back to the VA.

While Allan was annoyed, I was thrilled. As a social worker, I, too, wanted to be heard. Somehow, my words had crept through his earphones and burrowed into his brain. So often, veterans tuned me out, just as they tuned out others who told them hard truths.

A few weeks later, Allan disappeared. He went AWOL and took off overnight, but by then his sobriety time had increased from six to ten weeks. I could live with that, but could he? Would he?

I don't know. I never saw him again.

Trevor Revisited

The recovery world revolves around AA clichés: "One day at a time." "Easy does it." "Make amends." "Keep coming back." "It works if you work it." "Relapse is part of recovery."

Over the years, I came to believe in them. Some of them. Sometimes.

Two years after he graduated from the Domiciliary, I spotted my former patient, Trevor—who had completed no fewer than *thirty-three* drug rehab programs—on VA grounds. He still looked sleek, his dark African American skin and shaved head glistening in the morning sun, the blue jeans and white tee-shirt still neatly pressed. He waved, smiled, and, stopped by for a quick hello before catching the bus to Westwood, a half-mile northeast of the VA. How was he? "Blessed." Where was he living? At the California State Veterans Home on VA grounds (where I would later work). What was he doing in Westwood? Studying at the University of California, Los Angeles (UCLA). Trevor had just completed a ten-week course in chemical dependency studies. He would soon be handed a counseling certificate. Better still: This veteran now had more than a year's sobriety—the one qualification that he had always lacked.

Chuck Revisited

Chuck, the Vietnam veteran who had been happily homeless in downtown LA—fifty-something but still boyish, the charmer who wrote essays about why he didn't believe in AA—had a much harder time after leaving the Domiciliary. He had grown attached to me. "I'll miss our talks," I remember him saying, lingering in the doorway. Chuck was going to the Russ Hotel, a transitional housing program on Skid Row.

For thirty-two years, the street had been his home. He insisted he would be "fine" living in the area, especially under a roof, but when it was time to leave I could feel his fear about returning to "the jungle where I did crack." As a result, we agreed to meet once-weekly until he felt more secure. It was a promise I didn't expect, or dare to hope, Chuck would honor. To my surprise, he showed up a week later, on time.

It was that rare LA thing—a day of heavy rain—so he arrived cloaked in a large, black plastic garbage bag used as a raincoat, a hole punched through the top to make room for his head. Despite the rain, he carried a boom box which he clung to like a teddy bear: "It goes everywhere with me." Things were "kind of hard," he admitted, but he still wanted to stay off the streets. Chuck seemed to enjoy feeling like a respectable citizen, even a gentleman. Coming and going, he kissed my hand.

The next week he came again, but in an altogether different mood. Sighing, he sank into a chair, slapped his hands against its wicker arms and said, "I've gotta leave the Russ Hotel! I'm afraid to leave my room." The first week, he didn't step outside for fear of what he would find: The freeway underpass where he used to sleep. The friends who would resent him if he refused to buy their drugs.

I was confused. Hadn't this veteran said he would be comfortable in this environment, where he had lived for thirty-two years?

"Yes, but it was different," he explained. "I was in a fog then... a crack fog."

The next two weeks, he failed to show up. Word among the vets spread fast that Chuck "went out" (vet-speak for relapse, as in lost in space, or the twilight zone). Once again, I was sad, although not for long. Chuck had stayed off the street two weeks—for the first time in thirty-two years. And I heard, about six months later, that he was processing into a VA Supported Housing apartment. Would he be able to maintain it? Maybe not. Still, this was progress: Chuck was no longer content with life on the streets. He was brave enough to try living on his own, inside. He still had a dream.

Not a Stayer

He made me laugh.

He was Santa with a buzz cut: Thomas C, age fifty-three, jolly and rotund, with blue eyes almost the same color as the tee-shirt that didn't quite cover his formidable front.

Since 1996, Thomas had been a successful professional craps player in Las Vegas. Gambling, he said, was "a good life." But now, saddled with some overdrawn credit and brush-ups with collections, he was rethinking things. The guy also had a history of assaults against "Vegas types" as well as police.

Although his chart outlined a history of depression, Thomas laughed it off as a normal response to "being in a cell." Point well-taken. And to what did he attribute his current, upbeat mood? "Not being in a cell." He denied any need for mental health treatment. A well-meaning psychologist tried to persuade him to enter a highly regarded gambling treatment program in Cincinnati. "Too cold!" he said, affecting a mock shiver. "I like California and Vegas."

Indisputably, the guy needed long-term, intensive treatment, but the social work ethos is to guide, not lead. I wouldn't think of sending this man who loved sunny southern California and Las Vegas to Cincinnati in winter.

About a week after admission, he left the Domiciliary but at least had the courtesy to let me know beforehand. "I'm not a stayer," he said. "That's why I never got married."

Have a Heart

Had he not seen that veteran in the throes of a PTSD flashback during the "Seeking Safety" group, he probably wouldn't have come to see me.

Like many Vietnam combat veterans, Julio, now nearly seventy years old, had spent decades trying to forget the trauma of war. This was his fourth Domiciliary admission for alcohol abuse—a demon he was willing to face, unlike the ghost of PTSD. Usually quiet, this chubby Hispanic man, married with three grown children, retreated within himself and kept his emotions suspiciously under wraps. But after the "Seeking Safety" outburst he needed to talk.

Julio had a lot to unload. He described lifting dead bodies under the arms and dragging them to the side of the dirt road in Vietnam. He remembered how sometimes their brains "shot up" and splattered on his chest, even his forehead once, from the pressure of being dragged. Most memorably, he recounted, with obvious pain, his buddies' unique method of retaliating against a Vietnamese soldier who had killed fifteen Americans. "Does he have a heart?" they asked, laughing at their new captive. Then four or five of them assaulted the soldier, and began to cut out his heart while still alive. Julio objected, he said, until one of his comrades held a gun to his head and said, "SHUT UP!"

Forty years later, he held onto that nightmare. When undergoing heart surgery, Julio swore that "I could feel the pain, even with anesthesia. I wanted to scream but I couldn't." Once conscious, he found himself sobbing in the recovery room. This, he believed, was retribution for standing by while his comrades cut out the Vietnamese soldier's heart.

Whether or not this truly happened—it seemed incredibly ghastly—I can't say. But clearly, it was a true memory, one that felt real enough to make for forty years of suffering. Having survived the horrors of combat in Vietnam, he had plenty of experiences to ignite his imagination.

Julio was in the printing business. It was he who, many months later, worked with a psychologist on staff to compose that letter of support on my behalf following my expulsion from the Domiciliary. Among the sentiments it expressed: "Where there is only speculation that she has been disciplined, please do not let this be true and give us some assurances that it is indeed speculation. Mrs. Plate fully supports veterans in their recovery…"

It was Julio who led the effort to round up thirty veterans' signatures, attach it to the back of the letter, and present me with a laminated copy at the Opiate Treatment Program, in building 257, where I then worked.

Julio had a big heart. And I still have the letter.

Lost and Found

I never met this veteran, but I felt like I knew him.

I knew his son, Jake, a bright kid in his junior year at Loyola Marymount University. Jake was charming and cute, with long, wavy brown hair; a winning smile, and three years of experience as both full-time student and part-time pool boy at a posh LA hotel. His assignment, for my course on "Gender and the Military," was to interview someone who had served in the Armed Forces.

Jake wanted to write about his father, whom he described thus: A Vietnam combat veteran. A severe alcoholic. A husband and father who took off one day and never returned, leaving behind a family of three. Jake knew little more than his dad's first and last name.

Facebook, in its most benevolent form, does in fact help people connect.

That's where Jake found his father.

According to his essay, they talked on the phone about the veteran's excessive drinking, his deep depression, his impulsive but steadfast abandonment of his wife and sons. The experience was far from cathartic. But as Jake wrote: "At least I know who my father is. And I can tell my children and grandchildren."

Chapter Eleven

THE END OF THE TOUR
JUNE 2017

No Room for Combat

"The combat trauma program is full."

These were the words of "Nurse Ratched" (named after the stiff-lipped head nurse in the movie "One Flew Over the Cuckoo's Nest," played so convincingly by actress Louise Fletcher). She was a mid-level administrator, and was referring to the bed status on the second floor of building 217, home to forty returnees from Afghanistan and Iraq. The other five floors in the two Domiciliary buildings housed female veterans and men whose chief treatment problem was substance abuse or homelessness, or both.

Nurse Ratched conveyed the information as I was about to interview the first of four candidates applying for admission to the Domiciliary. I feigned surprise. How could it be "full"? We were still sending troops to Afghanistan and Iraq. But in truth, I knew the problem: The forty beds allotted to the combat trauma program were far too few for the number of mentally disturbed veterans returning from a theatre of operations. This was morally wrong. And absurd.

She handed me the mint-green slip of paper detailing bed availability: substance abuse, 4 (beds available); women's track, 1; combat, 0. "There aren't any available beds."

Sure, there were. As program manager of a substance abuse team, I knew the head count on each floor. The Domiciliary had 280 beds. At least two dozen were unfilled. So if the combat trauma track was reportedly full, "house" a combat veteran on a floor—any floor—with empty beds! That way, he could join the combat vets on 217-2 for programming, but sleep on another floor. Unthinkable! Too confusing! That's not how things are done! In other words, better to turn the veteran away than make an administrative adjustment.

The first interviewee that morning was in fact a combat veteran, age thirty-two, back from Afghanistan and eager for help. He had heard about the combat trauma program for young vets. He suffered from alcohol abuse, but it was the combat trauma he wanted to focus on first: "That's what keeps me up all night." How could I tell him the program was "full"? Communal living, shared experiences and a sense of belonging are key components of treating these young men. As their psychologist would say: "The milieu is in itself healing."

The vet continued to plead his case. Eyes alternately downcast and pleading, he insisted on the combat program, or he wouldn't enter into treatment.

I would not turn away this earnest young man. Defying Nurse Ratched's orders. I told this combat vet he could participate in programming with his peers but would sleep, and watch TV, on another floor. Happy, he left for a few days to await his admission. Meanwhile, he'd crash in the apartment of a friend.

That morning I had interviewed, and admitted, three vets needing treatment for substance abuse. It had been a grueling three hours—vets crying, yelling, saying they were "ready for treatment," but... then... not so sure ("Can I wait a couple of weeks?").

It was 11:35 a.m. I was done with all four. Nurse Ratched was in her office directly across the hall. Her door was open. She was on the phone. I tiptoed in, lightly dropping the big green admissions book on her desk. Unfortunately, she hung up and perused the list of new admissions before I could jet out the door.

Then hell broke loose.

"You are putting people on the wrong tracks!" Nurse Ratched said.

"No," I told her. "The placement is correct. It's the bed configuration that's wrong. That's *their* problem." I pointed left, to the end of the hall, inner sanctum of the Chief and Assistant Chief of the Domiciliary.

"You can't do that!" said the nurse.

"I just did," was my reply. "And I'll do it again until this admission and bed assignment deal is fixed."

"We have a process," said Nurse Ratched. Her thin lips grew thinner as they settled into a smug grin.

"Fix it, or take me off of screening duties!" That was my bottom-line.

No such luck. At the VA, hard work and sound judgment are the only defense against the constant onslaught of madness. It was just like that time in the ER, when I made the facetious bargain with that supervisor who telephoned one morning, after a harrowing night shift, to complain about three bus tokens which had disappeared on my watch. They would tolerate my sass—up to a point—because I could do the job.

In the end, Nurse Ratched telephoned this particular veteran at home to advise him that he would not be admitted to the combat track because there was no room. Instead, he would be placed on a substance abuse floor.

The veteran did not enter treatment.

What happened at that point? Only the veteran would know, but about a half-year later, when there was in fact an available bed on the combat trauma treatment floor, the returnee from Afghanistan was assigned to it and slept there for months while engaging in treatment.

This episode planted the seed in my brain: Maybe it was time to leave the VA. The pay and benefits packages were good. The job was steady and secure. To keep it, all I had to do was… what I believed to be wrong. That didn't seem right.

A New Commander

I had another epiphany on Inauguration Day. The VA was woefully understaffed, even as President Obama and Congress poured in additional money and posted more jobs. Under the Trump administration, wouldn't it be worse for both veterans and staff? The VA was declared exempt from the federal hiring freeze, but when staffers left, they often weren't replaced or it took years before the slot was filled. Since my departure in June of 2017, and at the time of this writing, numerous social work positions at the Domiciliary remain vacant. Indeed, in January 2019 the VA had 49,000 staff vacancies nationwide.

I couldn't possibly do any more with any less. And I did not want to suffocate in the tightening VA stranglehold. Inevitably, vets would be underserved: Waitlisted too long for appointments. Turned away for services. Told "Sorry, we don't have enough providers to offer individual counseling, or family support" (the clinicians were too busy with computer notes). I did not want to be part of this.

Not since George H.W. Bush have we had a President who served in the military. President Clinton dodged the draft. President W. Bush was in the Reserves. President Obama did not serve. President Trump was deferred due to bone spurs. I once led a "Straight Talk" group on this topic: Should military service be a requirement for the presidency? The vets in group that day didn't think so, but they thought it might help.

Because you have to see war, and serve in the military, to truly know it. Because you have to *feel* those experiences to understand them. Because to fairly evaluate the pros and cons of military intervention you need not just foreign policy expertise or an excellent

Cabinet, but muscle memory that sends commands from the battle-field to the hearts and brains of decision-makers. Would a president who served in the military have pardoned the notorious Bowe Bergdahl after his desertion? Or commuted the sentence of trans-gender Private Chelsea Manning for espionage? Or ordered troops into battle without a clear exit plan? This is not a left- or right-leaning question. It is a question of what is best for the veterans—some of our truest Americans, many of whom, alas, have been crushed first by poverty, gang life, violence, parents on drugs, lack of funds for education… then by the military.

Make Way for Ducklings

If sixty is the new thirty, this does not apply to the VA. Middle age is old. By the time I left in June of 2017, no one was hired or promoted inside the VA who had lived through the Vietnam War. Never mind Korea or WWII. I knew several Vietnam combat veterans who chose not to engage in therapy with a counselor the same age as their children or grandchildren. One said to me, "How can I explain to her what it felt like to come home to this country? When I mentioned 'baby killers,' she had no idea what I was talking about."

The good news is that the younger generation of social workers is being trained in all the right treatment protocols to manage the young men who served in Afghanistan and Iraq. But do they know American history? Military history? Do they realize that the effects of wars ripple throughout society a full forty years after they conclude? That's what former VA Secretary Robert McDonald told us when he visited the West Los Angeles VA.

The High

I have always been a geek. My parents didn't pay me to get good grades. I loved learning, which boosted my grade point average if not my popularity in high school. The "in" girls were the mean girls, the great dressers, the ones with nose jobs—not the bookish and politically inclined.

For all the travails, I found an immeasurable richness in being of service to veterans. Every day, I disappeared into the lives of others, blanketed by their anger and pain, unswervingly focused on getting veterans through the day, hidden deep within the barracks, away from civilian life. Every day I felt like Dorothy, swept up from my comfortable but limited life (Beverly Hills, not Kansas!) and dropped into a Land of Oz where there was no rainbow or yellow brick road, but magic in the mundane: bright eyes and smiles following a hot shower and a hot meal; minds that grow increasingly clear as they emerge from clouds of crack; and the confident strides of veterans heading to work rather than shuffling in line for a government hand-out.

And yet, that's the least of it. Selfishly speaking, this line of service was fun. I'm an adrenaline junkie. I loved the steady shocks and surprises; the flirtation with danger; the challenge of trying to keep grown men from falling into despair. And the longer I'm away from the institution, the fonder my memories. I can forget about the place, but I will never forget the thrill of working with veterans.

Close Encounters

The veteran Trevor, just about certified to work as a chemical dependency counselor, the two men who completed Domiciliary treatment and maintained steady jobs at the VA—they are obvious success stories. And yet, there were many other glimmers of hope.

I was working the phones one day up front at the Welcome Center when a vaguely familiar face appeared. "I'm Wally!'" he said. "What are you doing here?"

He thought I was still at the Domiciliary. That's where we met, ten years earlier, when he was in treatment for alcohol abuse. He, too, had a VA job. I can't remember in which department, doing which job. He told me, but the sight of this guy, more than a few pounds heavier and many years later, wearing a tan blazer and a straw hat over his dreadlocks, fill me with joy.

A few months later, I was at HR, trying to ignore the eye-rolls, sneers and other gestures of exasperation from the man behind the counter on hearing my request for a replacement VA badge holder. The old one, a lariat made of cloth, had broken apart. This was serious for two reasons: (1) We were told at every social work meeting: "You must wear your badge at all times! Above the waist so that everyone can identify you!" (2) It was a special lariat, one that would break in half should a veteran try to strangle you. (Neck jewelry was not advised.)

It was 1:03 p.m. Three minutes after lunch break. Twenty people were already in line. In just seconds, the man behind the counter could have plunked down a new badge holder. No chance! I had to wait, just like everyone else (But what about the vets waiting at my office?).

Then a voice rang out: "Mrs. Plate!" It was Jared, a former patient I hadn't seen, or heard from, in seven years—except for an email invitation to a tuba concert he gave at a community college (I didn't go; after-hours were reserved for recuperation and escape). Now he was working upstairs in HR. No doubt I would have gotten the badge holder more quickly, and certainly more courteously, had I asked him to intervene.

I remembered this forty-year-old veteran crying about his childhood in foster care, and I remembered my worries when he suddenly announced that he met a woman, fell in love, was about to get married and was leaving the program—so quickly! That kind of premature departure often signifies what's called a "flight to recovery," meaning, the patient convinces himself that he is cured so as to justify leaving treatment. Not this vet. He was grounded. He was still married and playing the tuba when he had time after work. Success!!

A few years earlier, I was at Cedars-Sinai Hospital in West LA, having pizza before a nighttime lecture on the subject of addiction among medical professionals. "Andrea Plate," a voice said as a hand touched my shoulder. It was Ken W. I remembered him instantly— the pale African American complexion (he was part Caucasian), the beautiful, light-gray eyes that made him look half-wolf, half ladies' man. What was he doing there?

"Learning," he said, introducing me to his fiancée. Then he explained that together, they ran "a sober coaching service." Several years later he closed the business to work in the field of high-end cars. Here was a man who, only years earlier, had worked as a pimp and limo driver, paid in cocaine.

This depth of rehabilitation happens all too rarely, but when you find it, and see it, it leaves an indelible impression on your heart.

These sober men are my heroes—not just for their successes, which are truly remarkable, but for the miraculous fact that they continue to try. True recovery is a lifelong marathon, measured in increments of twenty-four hours, and these men are off and running every day.

June 30, 2017

I had no regrets upon leaving the VA—perhaps because I took so much with me: Hope. Memories of courageous veterans and staff. Gratitude toward those men and women who gave me their trust.

Those who have relapsed repeatedly are also my heroes because they, too, try every day. I've met plenty of hotshot business execs, lawyers, doctors and politicians who don't have half the measure of self-awareness as these veterans—like the well-known judge who knocked over a bottle of wine at a high-class eatery, boasted about his ability to drive drunk without crashing the car and praised his wife for waiting at home, praying he was alive and making no negative comments when he entered the house.

Some of my guys have died. Many are still using. But they still try, against all the statistical odds, and their social workers try with them.

They still have hope, and so do I. If I learned nothing else in those fourteen-and-a-half years at the Department of Veterans Affairs, it was this: There is always hope.

Appendix

TEN COMMANDMENTS FOR SERVING AMERICA'S VETERANS

(1) We who send them far away to fight our fights must do a better job of fighting their fights when they return.

(2) "Leave no man behind" is heroic military creed but it rings hollow if we don't follow that advice ourselves when establishing programs and placements to help them heal.

(3) Success is helping a veteran, however you can.

(4) The higher up the chain of command, the easier it is to forget whom you are serving.

(5) Social work on behalf of veterans is more than a job; it is a passion.

(6) Make your decisions based on fact, but never forget that the heart is sometimes rightly decisive.

(7) Bureaucracy needs to enable better care, not just enable bureaucrats.

(8) Quality professional training—and retraining—cannot be under-rated.

(9) Failure is always a possibility but should never be seen as an inevitability.

(10) We who know the VA's imperfections need to fix it, and to elect politicians who can.

ACKNOWLEDGMENTS

I wish to thank Keith Korman for his dedication, enthusiasm and careful perusal of the manuscript of this book.

I am grateful to all those at the Department of Veterans Affairs who stood by me in the trenches, as well as at home, while writing this book, especially: Beverly Haas, PhD and VA psychologist; Michele Hargrove-Fouts, Julie Wright, Archer Parham, Gilad Dakik and Arrowa White, all wonderful VA social workers; Constance Nemec, a VA nurse practitioner for decades; Bill Pike, Vietnam combat veteran and dedicated volunteer working with veterans; Priscilla Garza-Stewart, my UCLA battle buddy in the Master of Social Work Program; and David Riley, LCSW, who hired me for that first VA job over the phone. They, too, are warriors worthy of our recognition.

Finally, many thanks to students, faculty and staff at Loyola Marymount University for their enthusiastic support of, and engagement in, my classes on the topic of America's veterans.

ABOUT THE AUTHOR

 Andrea Plate is a Licensed Clinical Social Worker (LCSW) by the state of California. She was a Senior Social Worker at the West Los Angeles branch of the U.S. Department of Veterans Affairs, within the Veterans Health Administration (VHA), for almost fifteen years.

Ms. Plate holds a Master's degree in Social Work/Public Policy from the University of California, Los Angeles (UCLA); a Master's degree from the University of Southern California (USC) School of Journalism; and a Bachelor's degree in English Literature from the University of California, Berkeley.

She teaches "Gender and the Military" at Loyola Marymount University in Los Angeles, where she is also a writing and editing instructor for its Asia Media International website. She has taught at Fordham University in the Bronx, New York; USC; Santa Monica College; and Mount Saint Mary's College. She is the author of two non-fiction books and has written magazine and newspaper articles.

As the child actress Andrea Darvi, she appeared on many television shows during the Golden Era of Television, including "Combat!", "The Twilight Zone" and "I Spy," and has worked in films with historic leading lights of the American movie industry, including Alfred Hitchcock, Richard Donner, Barbara Stanwyck, Danny Thomas, Gilbert Roland, Boris Karloff and Art Carney.

She considers helping veterans her best and most meaningful work by far.